THE
CODE
RED
REVOLUTION

THE CODE RED **REBEL MANIFESTO**

You are extraordinary! Do you know that?

The media, the food industry, the diet industry...

They all want you to believe there's something wrong with you.

That you don't have enough willpower.

That you have the wrong genetics.

That you'll never be enough.

But you are strong.

And you're invited to STAND AND JOIN OUR REVOLUTION.

We're taking back our lives, and we're doing it our own way.

Thousands of men and women who say NO MORE!

Being a Code Red Rebel is all about taking your life back and REBELLING against the rules you've been told to follow, like exercising the weight off and losing pounds slowly...

WE'RE REBELLING against pills, powders, shakes, GMOs, low-fat, artificial ingredients, manufactured franken-foods...

WE'RE REBELLING against the people who say, "It's genetic. You'll always be fat."

WE'RE REBELLING against the diet industry, which is always trying to convince you there's something wrong with you, and that this pill or that shake will fix it, if you'll just spend enough money.

WE'RE REBELLING against anyone or anything that makes you hate your perfect beautiful body! (Especially yourself.)

WE'RE REBELLING against the external search for willpower. You have all the power you'll ever need already inside you!

And **WE'RE JOINING TOGETHER** to offer support when one Rebel stumbles or feels weak.

We are **TAKING THE POWER BACK.**

We are **FINALLY TAKING CONTROL OF OUR LIVES!**

NO ONE gets to tell us what we should look like—not the TV, not the magazines, not YouTube, not the insurance companies, or the government...

NO ONE has the right to make us feel bad about our progress. Or tell us that we're doing it wrong. Or assume that we're going to just "gain it all back"...

No matter who you were before you joined the revolution, you are a new person now. You are whole and perfect and strong. You are a Code Red Rebel.

YOU CAN OVERCOME ANY CHALLENGE THAT STANDS IN YOUR WAY.

YOU CAN ACHIEVE YOUR GOALS.

WE BELIEVE IN YOU!

THE
CODE
RED
REVOLUTION

CRISTY
"CODE RED"
NICKEL

How Thousands of People are Losing Weight and Keeping it Off WITHOUT Pills, Shakes, Diet Foods, or Exercise

Print ISBN: 978-1-944602-09-3

Ebook ISBN: 978-1-944602-10-9

Thanet House Publishing

848 N. Rainbow Blvd. #750

Las Vegas, NV 89107

To order copies or inquire about corporate programs, contact: Sales@ThanetHousePublishing.com

Cover design and interior layout by Danielle Foster

Cover photo by Erin Blackwell Studio

Photography by: Chris Bennett and Erin Blackwell

Makeup by: Sarah James Eason

Publisher's Cataloging-In-Publication Data

(Prepared by The Donohue Group, Inc.)

Names: Nickel, Cristy. | Bennett, Chris, 1984- photographer.

Title: The Code Red revolution : how thousands of people are losing weight and keeping it off without pills, shakes, diet foods, or exercise / Cristy "Code Red" Nickel ; photography by: Chris Bennett.

Description: Las Vegas, NV : Thanet House Publishing, [2017] | Includes index.

Identifiers: ISBN 978-1-944602-09-3 (print) | ISBN 978-1-944602-10-9 (ebook)

Subjects: LCSH: Weight loss. | Low-carbohydrate diet. | Natural foods--Health aspects. | Lifestyles--Health aspects.

Classification: LCC RM222.2 .N53 2017 (print) | RM222.2 (ebook) | DDC 613.25--dc23

DISCLAIMER:

The author is not a licensed practitioner, physician, or medical professional and offers no medical diagnoses, treatments, suggestions, or counseling. The information presented herein has not been evaluated by the U.S. Food and Drug Administration, and it is not intended to diagnose, treat, cure, or prevent any disease. The information in this work is in no way intended as medical advice or as a substitute for medical counseling. The information should be used in conjunction with the guidance and care of your physician. Consult your physician before beginning this program as you would any weight-loss or weight-maintenance program.

Code Red Fitness & Nutrition, LLC provides the contents of this book on an "AS IS" basis and disclaims all representations and warranties, express or implied, including the warranty of merchantability and warranty for a particular purpose. You hereby release Code Red Fitness & Nutrition, LLC, its managers, members, employees, and agents for any damages whatsoever arising out of or in connection with your use of this book, including indirect, incidental, special, punitive, or consequential damages to the fullest extent permitted by law. Your use of this book confirms your agreement to the above terms and conditions.

More Weight-Loss Resources
From Cristy Code Red

FREE Code Red Starter Kit

www.CodeRedLifestyle.com/Print

The Code Red App

www.CodeRedLifestyle.com/App

The 10-Pound Takedown Challenge

www.10PoundTakedown.com

Personal and Corporate Wellness Programs

www.CodeRedLifestyle.com/Programs

Follow Cristy

Facebook

CodeRedLifestyle.com/Facebook

Instagram

CodeRedLifestyle.com/Instagram

Twitter

CodeRedLifestyle.com/Twitter

Snap Chat

CodeRedLifestyle.com/Snap-Chat

Contents

THE CODE RED PROGRAM

DIVE IN

REBEL FOR LIFE

Introduction

Does This Sound Familiar?

What's wrong with me?

Why can't I do this one simple thing?

Why does my body hate me?

Why was I cursed with this body?

I don't know you personally, but I'm guessing I've had clients just like you. My clients have struggled to lose weight for a long time, usually years and decades. Some of them tell me they've been heavy since childhood. They can't remember a time they weren't on a diet of some kind. Some of their past efforts were successful in the short term, but they couldn't manage to keep the weight off for good. All that failure weighs heavy on their hearts. They come to me in tears, desperate for a solution.

Their joints hurt. They're taking a long list of prescription medications to "manage" their health. They get winded walking up a short flight of stairs. They don't have the energy to play with their kids or grandkids. And some are afraid that if they don't get their weight under control now—they might not even survive the rest of the year. They are truly afraid they will die if they don't figure out the solution.

Now, it's not like these people haven't tried. They've tried everything! They've been on a dozen different extreme diets that required them to spend hundreds of dollars a month on special shakes and powders that tasted like garbage. They exercised faithfully for hours and hours—with pitifully little to show for it. They've taken all the pills, injected themselves with hormones and chemicals, and some have even had weight-loss surgery as a last result. None of these solutions worked for long. If they did initially lose weight, they inevitably gained it all back.

If any of this sounds familiar, you're not alone!

And most importantly...

There is hope!

When I work with my private clients, they are almost always at rock bottom. They have tried to figure it all out themselves and failed. They are ready to try something completely different! And they're ready to do whatever I recommend.

You're going to discover that my methods are different. They're scientifically proven, and the results my private clients get are undeniable. They typically lose 10% of their body weight every month until they reach goal weight. That usually averages out to between ½ and 1 pound gone every day! Best of all, they feel better than they have in years. They aren't hungry. They have tons of energy. And they know they can sustain the losses over the long term.

Does that sound unbelievable?

I get it. You've probably been told that losing more than 1–2 pounds per week is "unsafe." Bullcrap. It's totally safe. And it's not achieved by tricking your body chemistry. It's not achieved by punishing yourself with excessive exercise. It's achieved by lovingly feeding yourself real food, in the right proportions. It's achieved by getting lots of sleep and drinking lots of water—and a few other tricks I have up my sleeve.

When I help people lose weight, it's with the understanding that this is the **LAST TIME** they will ever have to do it! It's the **LAST TIME** around the weight-loss mountain. That means they're going to have to adopt some new mindsets and embrace some new ideas about nutrition. It also means they're going to have to reject what the billion-dollar food and diet industries have been telling them for decades. Because if someone is trying to sell you something, there's always a chance they'll lie to you to get your money.

So what about you?

Are you ready to take your life back and **MAKE THIS TIME THE LAST TIME**?

Before you're finished reading this book, I'm going to ask you to make a decision about that. But first, let me tell you a little about myself. I don't believe you should trust anyone without knowing at least a little about them.

My Fitness Discovery

Who is this Cristy Code Red chick, anyway? I've been in the health and fitness world for over 20 years. I've been a professional boxer, ranked #2 in the world at one time. I've been a celebrity trainer for people like Katie Couric and Peter Shankman. I've done a lot of things. But what I'm most proud of is helping men and women lose weight and take their lives back, even when they had given up hope.

I remember the first muscular woman I ever saw. I was 14, and a Miss Fitness USA competition came on one of the three channels we could watch on our old TV. I don't think they even have Miss Fitness competitions anymore, but back then they were pretty popular. My jaw dropped to the floor when I saw those women walk out on the stage. I had just never seen a muscular woman before.

My family lived in a tiny rural town of 2,000 people at the time, so there wasn't much local variety. We all looked like middle-America farmers. I could not get over how beautiful these women on the TV were. I was mesmerized. I didn't know anything about weight lifting or nutrition or anything. But I saw those muscles and I wanted them! Somehow, I was going to be that beautiful one day.

So I did what I thought would get me closer to that goal. I got a job cleaning up a gym. I cleaned mats, machines, and toilets. I was basically a janitor, but in my mind, it was where I needed to start to move closer to fitness. As time went by, I learned how to exercise and train, and after a lot of work, I became a personal trainer. More and more, clients came to me to lose weight. So I did what I thought was the right thing—I worked with them to try and exercise the weight off.

And it sort of worked. For some people. Some of the time. But the truth that I didn't know back then was that there's no way the average American is going to exercise off enough calories to make a dent in the amount of weight they need to lose. The government recommendation of "eat less, exercise more" just doesn't work in the real world. You're going to blow out a knee before you come even close to working off that caramel macchiato you drank before work.

That's how I discovered that the right nutrition is the key to weight loss, not exercise!

I've worked hard my entire life. It's just the way I am. One of my earliest memories is wanting my own horse. One of our neighbors had a beautiful Arabian, a bay gelding, just a breathtakingly beautiful animal. She knew I wanted a horse, and offered to sell the Arabian to me for $500. This was 1986, so not only was $500 a lot of money, but I was also only 10 years old.

Now, my family was poor. My parents hate when I say that, but we were. My parents didn't believe in credit cards, and running a farm isn't exactly lucrative, so I grew up with nothing. I remember my "cake" for my 16th birthday. It was a graham cracker with frosting my mother had made from sugar and milk spread on it. My sisters and I, we didn't get sneakers for basketball, we didn't go on vacations. We worked on the farm. I sewed my own prom dress. Every cent I made, I earned for myself. That's why I work so hard, because I know that if I want something, I have to get it myself.

So clearly there was no way I was getting any capital for the horse from my parents. But I wanted it. **I WANTED IT BAD!** So what did I do? I told our neighbor that I would pay her $50 a month over 10 months. And then I worked my butt off. I babysat, cut lawns, did everything I could to make $50 every month. That's a lot of dedication for a 10-year-old.

Once, the mother of the kid I babysat forgot to pay me. There I was, 10 years old, and I took this grown woman aside and explained to her that I had payments to make on a horse and she needed to pay me on time.

I paid for that horse in 10 months, and he was mine. His name was Ben, and to this day, he was the most beautiful horse I have ever owned. But he was only my horse because I worked as hard as I could to get him. I was completely focused on reaching my goal.

Anyone who tells you losing weight is easy is lying to you! You know it. I know it. They know it.

IT'S NOT EASY. BUT IT IS ACHIEVABLE!

And it can be the most rewarding journey of your life.

You absolutely can lose all the weight you need to—whether that's 10 pounds or 210—you just need to keep your eyes on the prize. Even though I had to wait 10 months for my horse, I believed it was worth all the effort. Losing weight, getting healthy, and taking your life back is absolutely worth the effort! **YOU ARE WORTH IT.**

Here's my promise to you: I have worked hard every day of my life, and if you stick with me, I will work just as hard to help you achieve your weight-loss goals.

The Critical Moment

When I was 18, I ran off with a guy. Growing up the way I did, college wasn't really talked about in my house. Anyway, I ran off with this guy, and not long into this relationship, he started beating me up. The abuse was physical and emotional. You know, being one of the premier female fighters in the world, I can take a beating. In some ways, the bullcrap he used to say to me took longer to recover from than the actual beating.

Each time, it got worse, and more than once he said he would kill me. One night, he beat me up worse than before. I remember waking up on the floor, just lying there in my own blood. It was, without question, the lowest point in my life. It was my rock bottom.

I knew I had to find the courage to get myself up off that floor and out of town, or I was going to die. I was physically and emotionally beaten down. It would have been easier to just lie there. The act of pushing myself off the floor, out of the puddle of my own blood was, to this day, the hardest thing I have ever done.

The reason I share this story is this: Everyone will face a time in their life when they feel completely beat down, and they won't know if they can push themselves up off that floor. You will have that moment—that critical moment where you have to make a decision. Get up off the floor and find a new way. Or lie there and bleed.

Rock bottom is different for everyone, and whether you're physically bleeding or just spiritually broken, it's all hard. I work with people who've reached that critical moment with their weight. It's do or die. They can't keep going the way they've been going for years. They can't be heavy anymore. And they'll do whatever it takes—if someone would just tell them the truth about what works.

This is your critical moment—the time to decide once and for all that you are going to lose the weight, no matter what it takes. The Code Red Lifestyle is how you get off the floor. It's hard pushing yourself off that floor. But I've done it. My clients have done it. And I know you can do it, too. It's worth the effort. **YOU ARE WORTH THE EFFORT.**

Life is always willing to throw a curveball. That's never going to change. Curveballs, challenges, obstacles—they all make you work harder. Holidays will come and go. Birthdays, weddings, vacations—none of them is an excuse to give up. Everybody makes mistakes. If you have a bad week and you slip and eat something you're not supposed to, I'll call you on it. But I won't give up on you. Giving up is one thing I will not forgive. If you quit on me, you quit on yourself. I can't help anyone who isn't willing to help themselves.

Commit like your life depends on it. Because **YOUR LIFE DOES DEPEND ON IT**. Approximately ⅔ of this country are overweight, and ⅓ is obese. Type II diabetes is at its highest rate in American history. Americans are on more prescription medication than ever before. The solution is nutrition—real, wholesome food to heal a body that's been abused with processed fake food for years.

Code Red is a lifestyle, and those who commit to that lifestyle are Rebels. Code Red Rebels eat nutritious food, drink a gallon of water, and weigh themselves, every day. Rebels log and measure their meals. Most importantly, Rebels don't quit.

I tell my clients to "pick their hard." The truth is, losing weight and changing your life with nutrition is hard. It requires commitment, honesty, and determination. At the same time, staying down on that floor, remaining sick and overweight is hard, too. Being overweight requires you to buy bigger clothes, sit out dances at weddings because your knees hurt, or not run around with your children. Staying down on that floor could even mean an early death. Both options are hard. Pick one.

People on my program get serious results because they're not just trying to lose weight. They are losing weight. They're getting healthy, ditching medications, and loving life!

If you're willing to push yourself off the floor and heal your life through nutrition, then I will be with you every step of the way. I will cry, sweat, and fight for you, if you commit to never give up.

You can do this. You are stronger than you know.

MAKE THIS THE LAST TIME YOU HAVE TO DO THIS!

Push yourself up off that floor and be a Code Red Rebel.

How This Book is Different

The Code Red Revolution is not just another weight-loss book—it's different. Most books and plans teach you one magical way to lose weight. They give you exact meals to follow. They prescribe a strict path to follow with Phase 1, Phase 2, and Phase 3. But they don't take into account just how wonderfully individual we all are.

This book is not only going to teach you how to lose weight and take your life back. It's going to show you how to **INTEGRATE THE PROGRAM RECOMMENDATIONS INTO YOUR DAILY LIFE**! Once you become a Code Red Rebel, you're a Rebel for life. And you shouldn't have to completely disrupt your life just to be healthy.

Maybe you're a stay-at-home parent who needs to cook for fussy eaters. I gotcha covered.

Maybe you travel for work and are rarely home to cook. You can absolutely learn how to eat in restaurants (from fast food to fine dining) every night, if you like.

Maybe you're allergic to certain types of foods. We can work with that.

Couch potato? No problem!

Vegetarian (or a really-hate-vegetables-tarian)? You can do this.

Code Red is all about taking your life back! That means living the way you want to, while still losing weight and getting healthy.

How to Read This Book

I know you're busy—you've got a life to lead, after all. So I'm not going to make this difficult. I've created this book to be easy to read, so you can learn a little or a lot and still get great results. The first few chapters are background information you're going to need on your journey. You need to know the truth about sugar, fat, and calories. You need to understand the difference between real food and fake food. You must understand what modern engineering has done to food in this day and age.

And what's the deal with exercise, anyway? Is it really possible to lose significant weight without exercise? (Yes!)

Then we'll move into the Code Red program itself. We'll go over the rules, the do's and don'ts, and some of the tools I use to help my private clients lose up to 10% of their body weight month after month.

One of the most important tools is your own mindset. If you've tried to lose weight in the past and failed, or gained it all back, then you get it. The program works almost like magic, but if your mind is sabotaging you at every turn—you're going to fail. So the first order of business is getting your mind and your body on the same page and working together.

Scattered throughout the book are little snippets of wisdom from our Code Red Life community. You'll hear from real-world Rebels who are losing weight and loving life. Community is a huge part of this program. You need to be connected with other people who are on the same journey. So you're invited to join us in Code Red Life by participating in one of our 10-Pound Takedown challenges. There, you'll get the support and accountability you need to be even more successful.

What Have You Got to Lose?

Of course, the whole point of this book is to lose weight, right? You're going to lose pounds and inches, if you stick with me. That's a given. But what else do you have to lose?

How about your CPAP machine? Would you like to fall asleep at night without a mask strapped to your face?

How about your diabetes medication? Or your blood pressure meds? Would you like to lose those forever?

Those pains in your knees, hips, elbows, lower back? Want to lose those, too?

Here's the deal—you're about to embark on a journey of healing. You're going to become healthy from the inside out. Humans weren't designed to need artificial help just to live. Joint pain and failing bodies are not a natural consequence of aging. They are a natural consequence of eating empty, processed, chemical-laden crap. They are a natural consequence of not getting enough water and sleep to rejuvenate your body on a cellular level. And they are a natural consequence of living in a stress-filled world.

I can't promise you that you'll lose all those things. (Really, the law says I can't promise that.) However, I've got hundreds of examples of real people just like you who are doing it. People I've seen do miraculous things when they set their minds and hearts on a path that works. They ate real food. They got lots of sleep. They drank lots of water. They didn't exercise themselves to death. And they were successful!

So take just a few minutes and think about what's weighing you down right now. Besides your extra pounds—what would you like to lose? Write them down. Then close your eyes and imagine for a moment.

What would it feel like to be rid of those things? Imagine yourself tossing that CPAP in the trash.

What would you do with all the extra money in your pocket once your doctor takes you off medication?

What new activities have you always wanted to try, but were afraid to?

What would it feel like to get through an entire day without pain?

Write it all out. Take as much time as you need. Don't skip this step. It's an important part of the process!

Before you can begin a journey, you've got to know where you're going.

Let's Make a Deal

Everything you're about to read is based on 20 years of working with all kinds of people. It's grounded in science, and it works. But I don't want you to take my word for it.

You've been fed so much bullcrap over the years from the diet industry and the fitness industry and the media. You've probably bought into lots of random weight-loss philosophies and been disappointed. I get it. Why should this be any different? Just because I'm declaring a revolution doesn't mean you'll actually lose weight. And just because you lose weight doesn't mean you'll keep it off forever.

So I'll make a deal with you, okay?

Read the whole book. I've tried to make it as easy to read as possible with small, easy-to-digest portions.

Pay special attention to the success stories. These are people just like you. They are mothers and fathers, grandparents, people with high blood pressure and diabetes, people who thought they had no hope. They found a way to believe in themselves. They followed the rules. And they were successful!

Read the whole book. Then try it out. Not just for a little bit. Dive in wholeheartedly.

Join the Code Red Life group on Facebook. Sign up to get my text messages every day. I've got your back, and I'll do everything I can to help you. (You'll find the instructions to sign up at the back of this book.)

I want you to see for yourself that this works. I want you to finally understand that you can lose weight predictably, without being hungry, without pills or powders, without spending money on weird diet foods, and without exercise.

You can do it. I know you can.

Then, once you've seen for yourself how well it works...

I want you to talk about it.

Share this book!

Tell your friends. Help your neighbors out. Get your family on board. Not in an obnoxious way. But when people see how well you're doing, they're going to be curious.

And they may be skeptical that it will work for them (just like you may be right now).

That's okay. Give them this book.

I'll do the rest.

I can't make a revolution happen all by myself.

I need you on my side.

Do we have a deal?

Awesome! I believe in you.

Natasha Hazlett

Lost 55 Pounds in 5¹/₂ Months

I REMEMBER the day I contacted Cristy like it was yesterday. I had hit rock bottom. I could not stand to look at myself in the mirror anymore. That day started with me in tears, but I ended it with a huge smile, because I made a decision that I knew would change my life forever.

My disordered eating started at the age of 13. My family members are all thin people, so I put a lot of pressure on myself to be thin like them even though I had a bigger frame. So I took diet pills and joined weight-loss programs like Jenny Craig and Nutrisystem—when I probably didn't even need to.

As a result of the diet roller coaster, I had an unhealthy relationship with food. I'd eat a ton for a few weeks, and then go on a diet. Then I'd eat a ton again, gain the weight back (and then some), and go on the next diet. By the time I got engaged, I was at my heaviest—I had gained 30 pounds since graduating from law school.

To prepare for my wedding, I started the Body For Life program, which had a nutrition component and a strict exercise regimen. It was awful because I don't like going to the gym. But since this was my wedding, I sucked it up and did the program. I hated every second of it, but I hit my goal weight.

After the wedding, I was totally done with diets. I had been on one diet or another since I was 13 and never wanted to think about my weight ever again. I decided that I was entitled to splurge because of my 14 years of dieting. Unfortunately, I "splurged" my way from a size 8 to a size 16/18.

My seven-year infertility struggle only exacerbated the situation because I used food to deal with that disappointment. I eventually ballooned up to 210 pounds. I can't fully express how ashamed I felt. I used to love to go shopping, but it became

a chore I dreaded because I was continually buying clothes in bigger and bigger sizes. It was humiliating. After each trip to the store, I would hate myself even more.

At that point I said, "Ok, Natasha. You've got to do something. This is getting out of control." So I put myself through 17 weeks of the South Beach Diet. After feeling hungry and deprived the whole time, I only lost a whopping 23 out of the 60 pounds I had gained. The thought of

having to suffer though another 6 months was unbearable. So I quit, and went back to my old habits.

My spiral toward the bottom started as I was planning my daughter's first birthday party. I was looking for pictures of me and my daughter to use at the party, and I could barely find any! I couldn't believe how hard it was to find photos of the two of us together—this beautiful baby I had prayed for and waited so long for. That's when I realized it was because I was ashamed of my size. I didn't want to be in the pictures, because I didn't want to "ruin" them by being so fat.

I feared that one day she would come to me and say, "Mommy, why aren't there any pictures of us when I was little?" What was I supposed to tell her? That I was ashamed of who I was? Because that was the truth. That wasn't the example I wanted to set for my daughter.

The sad reality was that when I looked in the mirror, I *hated* the person staring back at me. It sounds terrible, but I hated her. All I could think was *Who is this person? This is not me! What happened to me?* I didn't want to go out with my friends because I didn't want to be the fat girl in the pictures. My business was suffering because I hated being on video,

even though that's what I needed to do to continue growing our business. Bottom line—I was in a really dark place.

Then I ran into a friend who I hadn't seen in about 5 months, and she had *totally* transformed herself. She had lost close to 60 pounds and she looked completely different! I asked her what she had done, and she said, "It's just an eating plan. No exercise." I couldn't believe what I was hearing!

I followed Cristy on Facebook for months. When I finally reached out to her, I remember typing: "Ok, Cristy, let's do this thing. I'm ready to be the woman God intended me to be." That was it. I had made up my mind. No more excuses. I just needed someone to help me keep my commitment to myself.

drinking shakes, or buying expensive diet foods that taste like dirt.

I lost 55 pounds in just over 5 months. When people tell me, "Oh, you worked so hard for this. You deserve it…" I almost

Because of my dramatic weight loss, and the fact that I've kept it off, people want to do what I did. The funny thing is they keep saying, "Surely there are shakes to buy or pills to take, right? What about expensive food to buy?" I just say "NO! Just follow the simple rules and you'll get the results."

Once I signed up for a program with Cristy and I got the rules, I read them over and over thinking *That's it?! Really? How can this be possible?* The rules really are that simple. You just follow them, and you lose weight. No one had ever told me that I should skip the gym and get some extra sleep. Ever! It was so freeing to know I could eat real food and sleep and just live my life without taking pills,

feel guilty, because it wasn't hard. Sure, not having chocolate when I wanted it was a little hard, but I didn't have to go to the gym! Plus I knew I wasn't giving up chocolate forever, just for a little while.

The best part is that I now have the tools I need to stay healthy and trim *forever*. I can go on vacation and indulge. Then, when I get home, I hop right back on the program, follow the rules, and the 5 or

7 pounds I gained come right off! This is truly a lifestyle, not a diet. Finally!

Because of my dramatic weight loss, and the fact that I've kept it off, people want to do what I did. The funny thing is they keep saying, "Surely there are shakes to buy or pills to take, right? What about expensive food to buy?" I just say "NO! Just follow the simple rules and you'll get the results."

I still invest in Cristy's Hard Core Accountability program because being under Cristy's watchful eye is important to me. Although I lost my weight quickly, I've had an unhealthy relationship with food for years, so I need the accountability to retrain my brain and ensure that the lifestyle is ingrained in my DNA.

The Code Red Lifestyle has truly made me a better mother, wife, business coach, and friend. Now I'm not afraid to hop into pictures, or take videos for my business. And the ripple effect has been amazing. Some of my closest friends have worked with Cristy, and their lives have been transformed as well! In fact, over 50 of my friends joined up on Cristy's latest challenge—and they're getting awesome results!

People ask me all the time, "Do you think this could work for me?" I just want to shout, "Yes! Yes! Yes! If you're vegan, this will work for you. If you're pregnant, this

will work for you. If you're a man or a woman, old or young, if you travel all the time, or you like to eat out...it will work for you!

I can tell you with 100% certainty that I'm *never* going back to where I was. Fat, unhealthy Natasha is just not who I am anymore. Although I struggled privately with my weight for years, I decided to share my story publicly because I want to give a voice to people who are where I was—silently struggling with their weight. If you look in the mirror right now, and hate yourself, I know how you feel. You are not alone. You can do this, I promise. It's easy. It just works.

YOU CAN TAKE YOUR LIFE BACK.

I should know...because I just did.

MINDSET

1 Why We Carry Extra Weight

IT'S NATURAL TO GET ALL EMOTIONAL ABOUT OUR BODIES. After all, several billion-dollar industries are counting on us hating how we look. We've been brainwashed to believe there's something wrong with us ever since we could turn on the TV. Depending on how long you've been overweight, you may feel like your body is out to get you, like it's the enemy, like you're fighting a war. Often it feels like we're just outnumbered—our bodies are calling all the shots.

Why oh why do our bodies hate us?

Let's take a step back here for a moment and think. Your body is a complex organic mechanism. It completes thousands of processes just to get you through your day. And it takes energy to complete those processes, right?

Your body is designed to store energy, just in case at some point there is no food to be found.

Let me say that again. **YOUR BODY IS DESIGNED TO STORE ENERGY.**

It does that to keep you safe. To keep you alive when food becomes scarce. So you don't die!

That energy is stored in the form of fat.

Big deal, right? We all know that.

Well, consider this...

Maybe your body isn't the "enemy."

Maybe your body is perfect. It's doing its job day in and day out, regardless of how you feel about it.

You keep feeding it more calories than it needs for the day. It stores the extra in the form of fat, because someday you might need it. Only your body doesn't know that we live in an abundant society today. The majority of people have far more food than they will ever need. It's cheap and readily available any time of year.

We've become completely disconnected from our bodies. They go on about the work of converting the food we eat into the glucose (sugar) we need to survive, and storing whatever is left over. And we go on about our daily lives, shoveling in more and more food out of habit or boredom or anxiety—rarely because we're actually hungry.

What's really happening here is that we're storing up fat so we can survive during the next great famine. Except there isn't one. (Thank heaven!) So for years and years, we keep storing and storing. It's just a mechanical process. Yet we attach negative emotions to our bodies just for doing its job. It's hardly fair. But there is good news...

Your Body Has a Secret

Now what you may not realize is that your body is capable of running on two kinds of fuel—glucose and ketones. Sugar and carbohydrates break down into glucose, which is the easiest kind of fuel for our bodies to use. The process looks like this:

> You eat a bagel.

> Your body breaks it down into glucose and uses some of it.

> Whatever is left over is stored as fat for later.

This is an incredibly efficient process. Your body has been running on glucose most (if not all) of its life. It's very good at this conversion process, and it's very good at storing fat.

But what happens if you're suddenly shipwrecked and stranded on a desert island and have no access to starchy, sugary food? (Your cell phone drowned as you swam to shore, so there's no calling for help.) I call this the Gilligan Scenario. You can fish. You can hunt. Eventually, the professor in you figures out how to open a coconut. But that's pretty much it.

Would you die? No. Not from starvation, anyway. Not for a long time. Because you have all this glorious fat that your body has been storing up. Finally—it's time! Your body gets to do what it was designed to do—change its fuel source to ketones and use up some (or all) of the stored fat. Ketones are created from fat.

It's kind of like a hybrid car that can switch from electric energy to gasoline. You store gas in the tank for when you need it. The car runs on electricity until the battery runs dry, and then you just push a button and switch over to a different fuel source. Your body runs on glucose until there isn't any more available, then it switches over to ketones. It makes ketones by burning stored fat. The longer and more efficiently you burn ketones, the more stored fat gets used up. And the less you weigh!

Go back and read that last paragraph again. It will change your life.

Now, imagine you're back on the island, and you managed to rescue a water-proof crate full of Twinkies. (I don't know where they came from. Just run with it, okay?) Naturally, you're going to want to ration them. So you allow yourself just one Twinkie a day. The rest of the time, you eat fish and coconut milk.

Doing this, you're running on a little bit of both fuels. As you can imagine, it's not very efficient. Your body's engine never completely switches over to burning fat, so you just sort of sputter along. You're able to function. But you feel tired all the time. Maybe you have headaches and get grouchy.

This is what happens when you eat a so-called "healthy diet" by modern Western standards. When you consume foods that turn into glucose and foods that your body converts to ketones, your body is running on both kinds of fuel. Just not very well. It's also what happens when you switch back and forth between different diets, or when you allow yourself the occasional cheat. It's miserable!

Imagine for a moment what would happen if you could create the Gilligan Scenario on purpose, but in your own home, with showers and flush toilets and all your everyday comforts. What would happen if you chose to let your body switch fuels and burn fat for a while? What if you stopped feeding it grains and carbs and sugar, and switched to mostly healthy fat and protein?

I'll tell you what happens. Your body gets confused for a day or two. Is this for real? When is she going to go back to the bagels and doughnuts? Or should we think about switching over to fat? Hmm...not sure. Let's dump a bunch of water and see what happens. (The water flushes out and you lose several pounds right away.)

Then your body figures out that you're serious. The fuel source you're giving your body is high-fat and low-carbohydrate—perfect for creating ketones. Your body says, "Okie-doke! Time to switch over to fat-burning." And when you don't eat quite as much food as you need to survive, guess what?
IT BURNS THE STORED FAT!

It doesn't happen overnight. It can take a few days or a few weeks for your body to fully convert to fat-burning mode. But once it does, you'll notice your energy levels soar. That brain fog that's been holding you down for months or years suddenly lifts. And your weight drops. Continually. As long as you consistently feed your body what it needs to burn fat, it will! Whether you have 10 extra pounds of fat stored up or 250—your body will use that stored fat as fuel until you tell it to switch back to burning glucose.

Your body is perfect.

It's been doing its job all along.

The reason you've been unsuccessful losing weight in the past is simply because you haven't switched your fuel source long enough.

Again, your body is an amazing survival machine!

Its only goal is to keep you alive as long as possible.

So stop hating it, okay?

If switching fuel sources sounds simple, that's because it is. Stop eating bagels and doughnuts and start eating eggs and bacon. Let your body burn up the stored fat. Done.

If it's really that simple, why are so many people overweight? Why are there pills and powders and extreme exercise programs? Why do we make it so difficult on ourselves? The simple answer is money. There's not much money to be made by telling the truth. But there's a lot of money to be made by obscuring the facts and making things incredibly complicated.

I'm all about two things. Telling the truth. And keeping it simple.

This book is all about creating that Gilligan Scenario on purpose. Putting your body into fat-burning mode as long as necessary to drop all the weight you want. I call this "weight-loss mode" and its main purpose is to use up all the energy you've been storing for years.

Now, just because it's a simple process doesn't mean it's easy. You're up against billion-dollar marketing campaigns. You're up against possibly decades of hating your body. You're up against a stress-filled life, dealing with work and kids and pets and aging parents. My job here is to help you focus on the truth and immunize you against the advertising being pushed on you every day.

It's like that movie *The Matrix*. You get to decide. Take the blue pill, continue on the way you have been, and stay overweight. Or take the red pill and learn the truth. Take your life back forever. It really is as simple as switching your fuel sources and allowing your body to use what it's been storing for later.

Welcome to Code Red Club Med

People have two ideas about desert islands. The first is the idea of being stranded. Cut off from civilization. Sunburned and suffering from lack of food and fresh water. Literally wasting away from deprivation. Yes, you lose weight. But you're miserable! And as soon as you return to civilization, you go right back to your old habits and behaviors.

What if you flip that scenario and imagine that you're giving yourself a tremendous gift? What if you allow yourself to take the holiday of your dreams at a fantastic resort on a secluded and peaceful tropical island? Imagine yourself lying on a glittering white-sand beach that stretches for miles and miles. The clear blue water makes a quiet lapping sound at your feet as you give yourself permission to simply relax. Everything is just perfect. You have all the healthy food you need. You have an abundance of fresh, cool water. And there's plenty of time for sound, restorative sleep.

While you're on the island, you know you're going to lose weight. It's a given. But you don't have to struggle to do it. While you're there, why not try a nice yoga class? Or learn to paint? Or eat supper with a group of new friends? You can stay as long as you like. Until you lose all the weight you want. Or, if you like, you can simply live here forever.

Which island would you rather be "stranded" on during weight-loss mode?

Mindset is everything!

Here's the thing: When you tell yourself weight loss is hard, and you're going to be hungry, and you're probably going to fail, and even if you succeed, you'll probably gain it all back, all you're doing is raising your stress levels. You're releasing the fat-storing hormone cortisol into your body, and making all that doom and gloom come true. It's been proven over and over that weight comes off easier when your stress and cortisol levels are low. So why not just give yourself the gift of that tropical paradise?

Now you might be thinking, "That's great, Cristy, but you don't live in my world! I have a full-time job and three kids to take care of. And my mother needs my help constantly. My bills are late, and my boss is on my ass all the time to work harder. I don't have the luxury of taking a tropical holiday."

In that case, you need it even more! I'm not suggesting that you max out your credit cards and take an actual vacation from your life. I'm saying that your mind is powerful. And if you imagine yourself on that white-sand beach—even for just a few minutes before you get out of bed in the morning—your body will respond. You'll be more relaxed. You'll be able to handle your boss and your kids easier. And you'll find it's much easier to lose weight. Try it.

And in case you're wondering if this whole book is about "thinking the pounds away," don't worry. You're going to find some powerful information here. I just know that we've got to get your mindset straight first. Because once you make the decision that this is the last time you're going to do this weight-loss thing, everything works better.

Ryan Smathers

Lost 70 Pounds in 3 ½ Months (So Far)

BEFORE I FOUND the Code Red Lifestyle, I was just fat. There's no other way to describe it. I mean, I was always stocky and muscular. But about two years ago, I lost two close friends in an accident on the same day. That was so hard, and I think it was the tipping point where I just got really big. I turned to food and beer for comfort.

My wife and I both work, and we're very active in the community with our children. So most nights we wouldn't get home until eight or nine o'clock at night. We'd grab a frozen pizza or microwave whatever was in the freezer. I'd have a few beers and fall asleep on the couch. So of course everything I ate turned to fat.

I got so upset about my weight that I ended up on depression medication. I was

DEPRESSION, MEDICATION, AND MIGRAINES—GONE!

Luckily, my cholesterol was good, even though I was 100 pounds overweight. But my blood pressure was out of control. I took two different blood pressure medications every day, and it still wasn't enough. I suffered from migraines due to the high blood pressure, including two episodes where I lost my vision and the ability to speak.

I can happily say that after my first week of detoxing with Code Red, I have not had a single headache since. My blood pressure is now low, and I'm completely off the medication.

Overall, I've lost 70 pounds so far with Code Red, and it's only been 3½ months! People tell me all the time, "Well, that won't last! You'll gain it all back." And

embarrassed to go on family trips. When we were out on the lake, I was the guy who wouldn't go without a shirt. I was even starting to research all the surgical weight-loss options because I knew I didn't have the time or the willpower to diet. Diets wanted to take away everything I loved, and who wants that?

The biggest surprise to me was how simple this lifestyle is. We're all used to complicated diets with counting points and calories and exercising. With Code Red, you follow a few rules, and it just works. Don't try to make it more complicated than it is.

I just have to say no. No, I won't. If this were a diet, I might agree. But this is not a diet. It's a complete lifestyle change. I have the tools I need to keep losing until all 100 pounds of extra weight are gone, and I have the tools to maintain that loss. I'm never going back because this is my life now. And I love it!

One of the things I love about this program is that if my weight is up, there's always a reason for it and I can figure it out. This morning, for example, I was up about 2 pounds. On any other diet plan I can think of, it would be so easy to get discouraged and blame myself for "being bad." But the fact is, I ate well and drank all my water, but slept terribly last night. So I know the weight will be back down tomorrow as long as I stick with the plan and get to bed on time.

THE INCREDIBLE SHRINKING TOWN

The biggest surprise to me was how *simple* this lifestyle is. We're all used to complicated diets with counting points and calories and exercising. With Code Red, you follow a few rules, and it just works. Don't try to make it more complicated than it is.

My energy is through the roof. I look great in pictures. My whole family is getting healthier by the day. Even my 8-year-old reads nutrition labels now. In fact, much of our town is getting on board. I'm the mayor of our little town of Orofino, Idaho, and people watch me pretty closely. After seeing my success for the past few months, residents kept coming up to me and asking, "What are you doing?!" And I would just tell them it's the Code Red Lifestyle.

So they started looking into it and they've been adopting this lifestyle for themselves.

It's like a massive ripple effect happening. I think there are over 200 Orofino residents on Cristy's 10-Pound Takedown challenge right now, and I'm sure that number will probably grow in the future.

Everyone in town is talking about how great they feel. They're losing weight and smiling more! There's an infectious energy that just grows and grows. Who doesn't want to feel better? When you find something that works, you just have to share it.

One of the most astounding things is that the restaurants and coffee shops in town are actually consulting with Cristy and coming up with Code Red Approved menu items. The local businesses want to support us and help everyone live a healthier lifestyle. Our town is conforming to us, not the other way around. That doesn't happen every day.

Code Red is a life-changing choice. I could not be happier with the changes I've experienced.

2 Your Words Are Powerful

THROUGH THIS ENTIRE PROCESS, I want you to remember that this is all about you. You may have plenty of titles—spouse, mother, manager, sibling, whatever. But through this process, you have to focus on your health. Everything else will fall into place once you are taking better care of yourself. For this reason, I need you to understand the power of your words.

The power of the words you speak is very real. For example, if you go around telling everyone that you have high blood pressure, you are more likely to continue to have high blood pressure. The more energy you expend on that subject, the more real it is. Your words have the power to help or hinder you. If you constantly tell yourself that you can't do something, eventually that will be true. And you will have made it so.

For example, I am a very black-or-white person. I used to believe that I was not especially creative. I used to go around saying that to people. I would say that I wasn't an idea person, I was a follow-through person.

Finally someone called me on it. "Stop saying that, Cristy, it's not true." And I stopped to think. I paint, don't I? I am creative, and I do have ideas. So why was I attacking my creativity? Understanding the power of your words means being aware of your thoughts and not letting some of them become words.

The thing is, as soon as you speak words aloud, you are giving them power. If you're going to give words power, make them good words like "I can do this." Yes, you can!

We all struggle with negative, self-sabotaging thoughts sometimes. When that happens, just zip those lips. Ignore the thoughts and don't speak them out, because when you do, you're feeding that negative idea. Starve the negative ideas, and feed the good ones instead.

For those of you who are parents, you wouldn't let your kids sit there and put themselves down, would you? Don't put yourself down either! Think about what you are saying to or about yourself. If you wouldn't say it to your child, your parent, or your spouse, then you shouldn't say it to yourself. This is part of healing yourself and taking your life back. You are being good to your body by feeding it healthy, nutritious food. Be good to your mind too, and don't put yourself down, okay?

You know the old saying "If you don't have something nice to say, don't say anything at all?" That is a rule I want you to abide by with yourself. If you can't find something positive to say about yourself, at the very least don't say anything negative. We all have challenges in life. I am not asking you to ignore your problems, I am asking that you don't feed your problems by giving them a voice. The power of your unconscious mind is incredible, and you need to make sure it is on your side.

When I wake up, I stand in front of my mirror and say, "You are strong, you are beautiful, you are healthy, you are smart, you are creative." I say those words out loud. I thank God out loud for strong legs when I am running. I say thank you for my hip not hurting like it did last year. Focus on the positive in your life. Those are the words you need to give power and life to. You can tell yourself what you need to hear. You know you need to cut out the junk food; it's time to cut out the junk words. Give your body nutritious food, and give yourself wholesome words and encouragement.

Sheli Fulcher Koontz

Lost 35 Pounds and Is No Longer a "Heart Attack Waiting to Happen"

MY STORY is different from most when it comes to weight loss. I was always a small person. I'm only about 5′ 2″, and growing up I was always petite. Even into early adulthood, I was small, and never really had any trouble keeping in shape. I certainly never thought I would need to lose weight, let alone tell a weight-loss story.

My struggle with weight began when I became a mother. I had my child later than most people do, and I never got all the baby weight off. On top of that, I love to eat. Sometimes I would think the little switch in my brain that's supposed to tell me I'm full was broken.

It was a problem, though. My family has a history of pretty severe high cholesterol. I was working with an endocrinologist on gene therapy for my cholesterol, and he told me that the likelihood of my having a cardiac event wasn't a matter of if, but a matter of *when*.

When a doctor tells you that you will *have a heart attack or a stroke at some point, it really grabs your attention!*

I can eat *a lot*. But when I got into my 40s, I was eating like someone in their teens or 20s, and it caught up with me. I never felt fat unless I saw a picture of myself, or looked in a mirror. When I did that, I just hated what I saw.

My first attempts to lose weight were not successful, partly because I wasn't committed to whatever I was doing at the time, so the results were minimal. I would lose 5 or 10 pounds, but then I would stop, and gain it back. I justified it though. I told myself that I was just at "that age" where people gain weight. I hid the problem and pretended it wasn't there.

I met Cristy through a group of professionals in my community called the Rockstar Network and was immediately intrigued. She has this incredible presence...and a mohawk! I took one look at her and wondered, *What's her story?* She was very kind and engaging, so I followed her on Facebook for about 5 months before I decided I had to try something for the sake of my health. Even though I hadn't been successful with weight loss before, I took the leap and signed up for a one-on-one program. It was a lot of money, but I know that investment made me take the whole program seriously.

The program was simple, but at the same time difficult. We have sayings in the Code Red family and one of them is "Pick your hard." The program was hard, but walking around waiting for a heart attack was harder. Walking by mirrors and looking at myself in pictures was hardest. I needed to do it, and I am so grateful that I did.

SUPPORT IS KEY

I started my program on December 1st. I was not prepared for the lack of support from people who I thought would be in my corner. I had someone ask me, "How could you be so *dumb* to start a weight-loss program during the holidays?" I was shocked.

Someone else asked me, "What are you going to do when you gain it all back?" I was not prepared for the people in my life who were unable to be supportive friends. Looking back, I realize they were heavy themselves and not ready to make the change in their lives. So they felt the need to tear me down. But Code Red shows you that you are stronger than you think!

The support from Cristy and the Code Red family is simply outstanding. When you're making a lifestyle change like this one, it's worth more than gold to have that support group that you can take

your fears or struggles to. Cristy herself is really good at helping you field the haters, so to speak. Thanks to this group, I had an answer when that individual accused me of being dumb for starting a weight-loss program during the holiday season. I was able to just smile at her and say, "If I can be successful through the holidays, then I *know* I can be successful the rest of the time, too."

The relationships I've built among the Code Red Rebels have been amazing. I've made friends with so many wonderful people I wouldn't have met otherwise, all looking out for each other. I remember one woman who needed to go shopping for new clothes, and she hadn't ever shopped for "regular-sized" clothes before. I was able to meet her at the mall

and support her on this new part of her journey. And we had so much fun! That kind of support is part of what makes this program stand out from anything else.

GETTING OFF SUGAR

I won't lie—the first week was *horrible*. I never thought I had a sugar addiction, but detoxing off the sugar is a terrible experience. Quitting Diet Coke, bread, and pasta was not easy. I whined and complained. But Cristy was tough with me. Patient, but firm. I needed her to be firm, because I have a strong personality myself. She and I were a good match. She is so encouraging though, and she kept telling me during the first week, "Wait till Day 8. Once you get to Day 8, you'll feel like you've woken up."

She was right. Day 8 finally rolled around and I felt incredible. The headaches were gone, I had no pain, and I wasn't craving junk food at all. And for the first time I thought, *Okay, I can really do this*. From that day forward, I did *everything* she said. She monitored me and kept me on track, and battled with me to make sure I was successful.

I did notice that other people seemed to lose more weight faster than I did. That was something I really hadn't prepared

myself for. I'm naturally competitive, and wanted to be losing 2 to 5 pounds a week like the other Rebels. But I also didn't have as much to lose. My 35-pound journey was someone else's 60- or 100-pound journey. Cristy helped me see that comparing myself to someone else was devastating to my morale. I had to learn that any loss I had was progress, and there was nothing "wrong with me" because my journey was different.

TAKING MY LIFE BACK, FOR GOOD!

My family was great. My dad has been my number one cheerleader, to an embarrassing point. He tells people about my weight loss, because he's proud of me. My husband was worried about my health, so he's happy for the improvement in my life. He chooses not to eat the way I do, which is fine. And my son was my little accountability manager. He met Cristy and was very taken with her. From then on, he was always there to make sure I stayed on track. Whenever he thought I was going to cheat, or have something I shouldn't, he'd say, "Don't you eat that, it's not Code Red Approved. I have Cristy's number!" He was great.

Now, my son does not need to lose any weight at all, but he does have ADHD, so I adjusted what he eats a little bit. Nothing extreme, just fewer carbs and sugar with more fat and protein. Just that little tweak has really helped him out a lot with his behavior and attention.

At this point, I am 35 pounds down. I haven't been this small since I was 18!

In addition to being back to a one-digit dress size, I got good news from my doctor. My cholesterol has dropped 100 points! And that's while I was eating eggs, bacon, avocado, and coconut oil. I went back to my endocrinologist and told him the news. I expected him to be concerned about what I was eating, but he just said, "Whatever you're doing, it's working. Keep it up." I had also started taking Glucophage for pre-diabetes, and I don't have to do that anymore.

I do things now that I had stopped doing. I'm a den mother for the Cub Scouts, and now I can hike 15 miles with the kids when I used to only manage 3 or 4. I can walk up a hill or flight of stairs without seeing stars. I can look in a mirror without revulsion now.

I hadn't realized how much I hated myself until I made this lifestyle change. They say we're our own worst critics, and that was true for me. I used to call myself horrible names that I would *never* call somebody else. I have a new appreciation for myself!

Cristy talks about "taking your life back" and, while neither of us are touchy-feely kind of people, I can tell you that with her help, that is exactly what I did. I took my life back! It wasn't easy, but it wasn't any harder than hating what I saw in the mirror every day. I did it, because I *could* do it.

You can, too.

3 Create Your Most Powerful Weight-Loss Tool

SCALES ARE GREAT, MEASURING SPOONS ARE POWERFUL, but I'm about to show you the most amazing tool you have in your arsenal to meet any goal, especially weight loss: your own words.

Have you ever watched a reality TV show? You know, the ones where people go into a private room and record "confessional" videos? They might be funny or they might make you cry, but those videos allow you into that person's real thoughts and feelings. The best ones are raw and full of emotion. The same can be said for success stories in weight-loss and fitness magazines, blogs, and TV shows.

The fitness industry relies heavily on those emotional success stories to sell everything from pills and shakes to gym memberships and videos. We connect with success stories because chances are we're somewhere at the beginning. We can relate to the mom of three who used to be athletic but let herself get 40 pounds overweight. Or the bachelor who was always "the funny, fat friend" but could never get a date.

And what do we do when we read those stories? We feel like if they can lose the weight, so can we! We are in the same boat. If we just do the right things (or buy whatever that story is selling), then we'll be successful, too.

As powerful as those confessional videos and success stories are, nothing will ever be more empowering and inspirational than **YOUR OWN SUCCESS STORY**! That's right. Your before and after pictures. Your testimony about your own journey.

Here's the thing—only you know what will truly motivate you to finally lose the weight. **ONLY YOU KNOW YOUR WHY.** Maybe you just want to play with your kids without getting out of breath. Maybe you want to look hot in a bikini on your honeymoon. Maybe you want to compete in full-contact armored combat. (Don't laugh—that's a real client I'm talking about.) Deep down, you know why you want to do this. So let's tap into that well of inspiration and create a tool that will help you reach your goal faster than you can imagine.

I want you to create your own confessional video diary. Don't worry, no one is going to see it but you. All you have to do is go into a room (or maybe your car) and use your phone or a computer to record yourself. When you look into the camera, imagine you're talking to yourself. You are recording a message to the future you.

Now, Future You is definitely losing weight, but they might be sick and tired of this program. They're tired of measuring. They want to have a drink with the girls once in a while. They're ready to give in to temptation. They're about to go on vacation and completely blow all the progress you've made.

YOU are not going to let that happen.

YOU are going to give Future You a pep talk.

YOU are going to beg and plead for Future You to not give up.

You're going to do whatever it takes to keep yourself on track!

I know this might sound silly, but hang with me here, okay?

The first video will probably be the most raw and emotional. I want you to explain to the camera exactly how you feel at that moment. Before you start the program—before you've lost any weight—describe how you feel.

How does your body feel when you wake up in the morning? Does anything hurt?

Do you feel drained all day long?

What about climbing stairs or picking up your children? How does that feel?

What activities are you missing out on because of your weight?

What activities have you always wanted to try but haven't because of your weight?

How do you dress? Why?

And how do you feel on the inside? Are you hurting? Are you ashamed? Are you scared?

Is there someone you want to be proud of you?

Lay it all out for yourself! It's so important for you to **DRAW A LINE IN THE SAND AND SAY NO MORE**. You are never going back to your old way of life. You are becoming a new person, and you need to vividly remember where you started from. Your brain will play all kinds of tricks on you. It will try and sabotage your efforts. When you think back, your brain will make the details a little fuzzy. It will try and convince you that your heaviest weight wasn't so bad.

This video is your line in the sand. It's what you're going to come back to every time you think "it wasn't so bad." I want you to lay out your pain in great detail. It's not fun, I know. You're probably going to resist it. But trust me, in a few weeks or months, you'll be glad you did it!

After you describe how you're feeling at the beginning of this journey, I want you to start talking about your hopes and dreams. Tell Future You what you're looking forward to. What activities will you take up? What kinds of clothes will you wear when you're smaller? How will your life be different? Paint this picture in glorious bold colors! Visualize exactly how you will look and feel when you lose this weight, and speak it aloud on the video. Help Future You remember the dream when they're about to cave in.

Finally, I want you to give Future You a pep talk. Beg and plead if you have to. Tell them not to give up! Tell them it's not worth cheating, not even once! Tell them you are counting on them to stick with the plan. Tell them you believe in them, and you believe in you, and you know you can do this. Say whatever you have to, and say it with love.

That's the first episode of your video diary. It might be short or it might be long. All that matters is that you are completely honest with yourself. All that matters is that you speak from your heart and give voice to the hopes and dreams you've been hiding inside. You know, the hopes and dreams you've been stuffing down deep with food. Let them come to the surface. The words are powerful. Speak them.

The Rest of Your Video Diary

You've just created an amazing tool. Anytime you feel like caving in to temptation or you just want to give up, watch that video! Anytime you feel like your body has turned against you, watch the video. Anytime you just need a reminder of how far you've come, watch the video. Don't just record it and forget about it. Use it to motivate you and spur you on.

Future entries are up to you, but I encourage you to talk to Future You at least once or twice a month. Did you survive vacation without cheating? Awesome! Record an entry and talk about how proud you are of yourself. Did you zip up a smaller pair of jeans? Make a video! Record your celebrations and your setbacks. Record your ups and your downs. It's all part of the journey, and it will all help keep you going when you're having a challenging week.

There's one very important rule with your video diary—**NO NEGATIVE SELF-TALK**. It's not allowed! In your first "baseline" video, it's okay to describe how you're feeling, and a lot of it will probably be negative. But after that, you must treat your body and your mind with kindness and respect. Your body has one job—to keep you alive. And it has done that job perfectly! Talk lovingly about yourself. Even if you're frustrated, use kind words. They are powerful.

In fact, I recommend you finish every video by looking into the camera and saying, "I love you" and "Thank you for taking such good care of me." It sounds kind of hippity-dippity, but it's not. Even if you feel ridiculous, do it anyway. The more you get used to talking nicely to yourself, the more your body will respond the way you want it to.

Kevin LeBlanc

Lost 42 Pounds and No Longer Eats for Entertainment

I GREW UP very aware of body weight. My mother is extremely fit and my dad is obese. Opposites attract, right? That is the dichotomy I grew up with, and throughout my childhood and into adulthood, I have watched my dad struggle with his weight. He's tried more diets than I can name: Nutrisystem, Atkins, Weight Watchers, etc. He was usually successful too, losing anywhere from 25 to 40 pounds, but then he would put everything back on and then some. So watching him, I figured that Dad was heavy because it's part of who he is.

As for myself, I have always been average. Even through my teens and into early adulthood, I always liked to move, whether hiking, doing yard work, swimming, or taking long walks. Now I look just like my dad, right up to the male-pattern baldness (thanks, Dad), so on a subconscious level, I just figured I would end up basically being him when I grew up.

Therefore, when I started gaining weight after college, I just chalked it up to the process where I slowly turned into my father. I mean, I even chose a wedding band that could be resized, because I remember my dad having to have his cut off.

I used food as a reward, or held it over my own head when it came to things I had to get done. I would come home from work and tell myself that I wasn't going to eat until the dishes were cleaned and put away, the lawn was mowed, and the laundry was done. This contributed to my habit of eating late, because it would often take me a while to do everything I planned to do.

In addition, food was my number one source of fun and entertainment. If I had a free Saturday night, instead of going out with friends, I would bring a book to the Chinese Buffet and spend an hour or two there. Or I would just go home, pick out a few movies to watch, and spend three hours or so on the couch eating and watching Star Wars. When I turned 21, that entertainment expanded to include alcohol, so I was drinking and eating junk food late into the night, every night. In addition, I lived a dehydrated life. I would drink coffee from 6 in the morning until 5 at night, and then I would drink alcohol and soda from 5 p.m. until 1 a.m..

I repeated that behavior for almost 10 years.

The thing is, I didn't really think I was obese. I was fairly regular at the gym, and was lifting weights several times a week, so I thought I was just burly, you know? Knowing what I do now, I am not surprised that I became as heavy as I was. I'm 5' 11" and, at my heaviest, I was around 246 pounds. I am surprised that I don't have diabetes or liver cancer. I was terrible to my body. Dad is pre-diabetic,

> *The thing is, I didn't really think I was obese. I was fairly regular at the gym, and was lifting weights several times a week, so I thought I was just burly, you know? Knowing what I do now, I am not surprised that I became as heavy as I was.*

My wife has struggled with her weight for a lot longer than I have, and she and I would continually try to lose weight while the other was in a phase of "I'll eat what I want." She'd come home and say something like, "Honey, I want to do a 10-day cleanse" and I would respond with something like, "That sounds great, you totally should!" I was more than happy to encourage her from the sidelines while eating two cans of Pringles and washing them down with a pint of gin every night. Or, when I decided to try and make a change and suggest a chicken and kale salad for dinner, she was more in the mood for Chinese takeout.

so if I didn't change anything, I believe my future would have held that, too.

Fortunately, my wife's cousin discovered the Code Red Lifestyle. I watched her lose a lot of weight, in what seemed like no time. When she told me what she was doing, I was like, "That is too good to be true—it can't be that easy." She wasn't even exercising! She was just eating things like bacon and avocado, and drinking a bunch of water. It sounded too good to be true, but it also sounded too good not to try.

So in March of 2017, I decided to give it a try, and what's more, my wife did too.

For whatever reason, we both decided enough was enough at the same time, and we hit her cousin up for the rules. She was on one of Cristy's 1:1 programs, so we didn't get all of the custom formulated stuff, but we learned the basics:

- Cut out sugar and grains.
- Drink a gallon of water a day.
- Fats (except for trans fats) are good.
- Sleep 8 hours a night.
- Hold off on exercise.

(I was stoked about the last one because, while I would go to the gym, I never enjoyed the cardio, which I had always thought was what would burn my fat off, but it always made me feel even more fat.)

All we did was follow the rules. We told each other (and ourselves) that we were "just trying this out." Nobody had to do anything forever.

The results were, and continue to be, incredible to me!

Together, we have lost a combined weight of over 80 pounds. I was wearing size 38 pants that would just barely button, but now I am down to a size 34 with

room. My wife and I have each lost over 40 pounds, and we both continue to lose.

This is not to say that there were no adjustments that had to be made. I was pretty disappointed to find out that the majority of my bulk was not muscle, but carefully concealed fat. I didn't know fat could hide in my arms and pretend to be muscle! Still, I do not miss those 42 pounds.

I was never big on sweets, and I had mostly quit soda before finding out about Cristy, but I was totally ignorant of how much

snacking that was, and still is, the hardest change for me to make. I changed what I ate for snacks and greatly limited the amount of snacking I do, but in that hour and a half before bed, I still struggle with wanting to eat something while knowing full well that I don't need to. The rest of any given day is easy.

In the past, I never ate out of hunger; I ate for entertainment. The food I eat now is as filling as it is delicious, and I know that I don't need nearly as much as I think I want. That reset in the brain, switching food from entertainment to utility, has been my number one biggest challenge.

water I was denying myself. So while I didn't have to detox from sugar, I was amazed to see how good I felt drinking 7 fewer cups of coffee a day and not drinking myself to sleep 7 nights a week.

One big adjustment for me was not eating after 6:30 p.m. While the water was a challenge early on, it was the late-night

I can honestly tell you that finding out about Cristy probably lengthened my lifespan. I have had bad knees since I was 13, but now I'll save them some unnecessary wear and tear, weighing 40 pounds less. I can do burpees now, without thinking I am going to die. Most significantly, I have finally taken responsibility for my own future.

THE TRUTH ABOUT...

4 The Truth About Exercise

LET'S GET THIS OUT IN THE OPEN RIGHT NOW. Exercise is a wonderful thing. It helps your mood. It keeps your circulation stable. You should absolutely exercise. I was a professional athlete and got paid to exercise.

But hear me...

EXERCISE HAS NOTHING TO DO WITH LOSING WEIGHT.

I know some people reading this might be mad at me. A ton of money has been spent to convince you that you have to exercise off the calories. But my experience with actual clients proves otherwise.

For so many people, exercise has become some sort of sick self-torture. They punish themselves at the gym, and the more brutal the workout, the more virtuous they feel. Exercise is not a punishment. It's a glorious celebration of your physical ability. It's a thank you to your body for getting you through another day. It's a reward.

And you know what else? You're not "bad" if you skip the gym in favor of an extra hour of sleep. People are far more sleep-deprived than exercise-deprived in this country. And if your goal is to lose pounds, sleep will do you more good.

We have all heard that exercise is the way to address weight loss, right? But take a look behind the curtain for a minute. Who has been telling us this? Hmm, could it be the fitness industry? Could it be the very people who stand to make billions of dollars?

The whole idea is that exercise burns calories, right? So theoretically, if you exercise long enough or hard enough, you'll burn off that stored-up fat. Let me clear this up for you right now. You'll never be able to exercise enough to lose more than a couple of pounds without also managing what goes into your mouth.

You're more likely to blow out a knee before you lose any significant weight. You can exercise twice a day if you want, but if you eat a larger dinner that night or you eat a pickle with your cheeseburger, then most likely your weight will be up the next day, not down.

Exercise doesn't matter when it comes to weight loss. It's hard for me to say that, having studied exercise physiology in college. It's hard for me to say that, having made my career as a professional athlete, but it is the truth. I learned this when I was a professional trainer. I would put people through grueling workouts, but they never saw the results that my clients see now.

You will never outrun your fork.

You can't out-train a bad diet.

The trap so many people fall into is that they exercise really hard, but they don't have a solid nutrition plan or reliable coaching. After their workouts, they eat way more than they should, and when the scale goes up, they think they've put on muscle. They haven't.

It takes a long time to put on legitimate muscle, particularly for women. I carry much more muscle than the average woman, and I have worked at that for 20 years. Women simply don't have the testosterone to put on muscle as quickly as men do. Women are designed for childbearing, not for hunting and gathering. So women who want to carry more muscle will have to work harder for it. It takes steady, heavy weight lifting to really build muscle. Heavy dead-lifts, cleans, split and squats, and other heavy compound lifts are what people must do to put on muscle. The average person is not putting on muscle when their weight goes up.

There are two things happening when exercise produces weight increase. In the first week of exercising, particularly weight training, your body is hoarding water. When you lift weights, your muscle fibers tear, then they repair themselves while you sleep. Those repairs take water. And your muscles are going to hang on to as much water as they can, as a defense mechanism.

That first week of weight lifting can be a nasty surprise for people. Their bodies are holding on to all that water, and they get swollen. Pants that used to fit don't anymore, shirts get tighter, and it can be frustrating. After the first week, when your body realizes that the exercise is a normal thing now, that there's plenty of water and plenty of sleep, it will let go of the water and swollen muscles.

Over the long term, another problem arises—hunger. Exercise makes people hungry, and often people will eat more because they're hungrier. They'll justify it with the fact that they exercised hard that day. Or they just won't even notice that they're consuming more calories.

This is why I take people off exercise when they first start my program. The nutrition program is intense, and I encourage people to focus on that rather than exercise to avoid increasing their hunger. It's not as though weight loss is the only thing a person has to worry about. People have jobs, kids, marriages to manage, and often elderly parents to care for. Focusing on eating right is challenging enough in the beginning without worrying about exercise too.

When It Is Time to Exercise

All that being said, when the time is right, exercise is hugely beneficial. You will know when you are ready to add in exercise. Your body will tell you. You'll actually *want* to take a walk or play with your kids in the park. It might come as a total surprise. Like, who is this woman? Where did she come from?

For my private clients, exercise happens when they have gotten down to goal weight and they want to get rid of the jigglies. Welcome to weight training! The good news is that anyone can lose weight, and they can lose as much as they would like. However, here's another hard truth—you probably won't look really good naked unless you begin weight training. You can compare four women who are the same weight, and each one might have a completely different shape. That is body composition, and weight training is what allows you to alter yours.

One thing I hear all the time is "Well, I used to..." Anything can follow that. People tell me they used to do CrossFit, they used to kickbox, they used to do kettlebells. I think it's great that people have some experience, but when it comes to getting back into shape, what people used to do doesn't matter all that much.

I love when guys say, "Oh, I was an all-star state champion in high school." That's great, but that was 25 years ago and you have high cholesterol now.

I don't want to be negative, but if you are out of shape, you have to start at the bottom—regardless of what you used to do. If you used to be an athlete, the good news is that your body will be ready to slip back into being athletic. Your body will remember how to exercise, but you still have to start at the beginning, or you're likely to get hurt.

You have to ease into this, or you'll do more long-term harm than good. What's the point of saying you ran 10 miles if you're too sore to do the same thing tomorrow? What good is it to lift heavy if you blow out your rotator cuff and have to have surgery and spend 6 months in rehab? Once again, **IT'S ALL ABOUT BEING HONEST WITH YOURSELF**.

What About Cardio?

Another thing I hear all the time is "I want to start toning. I don't like the bat wings under my arms."

Some people are convinced that cardio is the way to fitness. All that running, all that time on the elliptical or the bike—all that is great for your heart and lungs. It's okay to help you burn calories. But it is not going to tone you, build muscle, or help you lose weight. Don't get me wrong, a healthy heart and lungs are goals that everyone should pursue, but cardio is not the only thing you need to do.

Weight training burns calories long after you have put down the weights. It burns calories through the night. Cardio, on the other hand, only burns calories while you are doing it. If you're running on the treadmill and you cover 3 miles in 30 minutes, that's great. You burned 326 calories...and that's it. You worked your heart and lungs, and that is good for the overall goal of improved fitness. However, it will not tone jiggly arms or a droopy butt.

Here's the good news—you don't need to get a gym membership. Save your money. There are things you can do every day in your home for free. If you find that you can do every rep, every set, every day consistently, then perhaps you should look at joining a gym. But if you can't stick to an at-home exercise regimen, what makes you think you can justify spending $50 a month on a gym membership? You're looking at $140 a month for CrossFit. You don't want to hand over that kind of money every month unless you are showing

up regularly. That is why I encourage people to seek success at home before they pay to try it somewhere else.

You do have to start somewhere, though. I think your living room is probably the best place, and the push-up is the best exercise to start with. Push-ups are the single best exercise you can do, because they don't just use one muscle group. They work your chest, arms, abs, and thighs. You are working each of those muscle groups simultaneously with each push-up.

Don't worry if you aren't doing a "perfect" push-up. You can go as low as you feel comfortable going. I recommend 3 sets of 10. Breathe out on your way up and breathe in on your way down. If you can't do one full push-up, start them from your knees. If you can't do that, do them against the wall, with as much of an incline as you can handle. I do push-ups every day. They're amazing!

The other at-home exercise to start doing is the bodyweight squat. With your feet about shoulder width apart, squat all the way down, like a toddler. You might be thinking that your knees can't handle it, but that is because most people squat the wrong way. If you stop halfway, your knees will hurt because halfway is where the knees are at their highest tension. Follow the movement all the way down so you are sitting on your ankles. Then return to standing position.

This one exercise engages lots of lower-body muscles. When you're all the way down, you'll feel it in your bottom. That is how you know you're engaging your glutes. And that, my friends, is how you tone your body.

If I had to pick just two exercises to do every day for the rest of my life, they would be push-ups and bodyweight squats. They're excellent; they don't require any special equipment, and they are 100% effective. If you can do 3 sets of 10 of each exercise every day, you will be headed toward excellent shape in a short while. It really is this easy to transform your body.

You don't have to do Tae Bo or Zumba. You can if you want. Some people think Zumba is a lot of fun. If that is your thing, then good for you. But remember that you don't have to pay money to get toned. Just like you don't have to pay money to lose weight. With just these two exercises, you can get all the toning you need in your own home for free.

Whatever you do for exercise, it all comes down to consistency. If you can consistently do 3 sets of 10 push-ups and squats every day, then you are doing exactly what you need to do. It doesn't have to be Zumba, it doesn't have to be CrossFit, but it must be consistent.

Did you hear me? I'll say it again.

It doesn't matter what you do for exercise, as long as you do it consistently. That is how you transform and sculpt your body.

When you have achieved your goal weight and begin to see the positive changes in your life from exercise, you won't believe what you can do. I hear people say all the time, "I was never able to pick up my grandchild before, but now I can!" I love stories like that, and it doesn't take fancy moves or fancy equipment. It doesn't take a gym membership; it takes consistency.

If you have a bad knee, it's probably because you never exercise it. Start off with little squats and gradually, if you are consistent, you will be able to go lower and lower. You don't have to do perfect push-ups either. There is nothing wrong with doing push-ups from your knees. If you do them every day, you'll be doing regular push-ups before long.

Age isn't an excuse either. People tell me, "I'm not 20 anymore." Neither am I. If you start at the beginning and stay consistent every day after that, it will not matter how old you are. I have a client who is over 60, and she runs full marathons. Stick to the plan, make consistency your unbreakable rule, and **ENJOY YOUR EXERCISE**. It's a reward, not a punishment.

Erin Neuhardt-LeBlanc

Found a Sustainable Way to Lose 43 Pounds and is Still Steadily Losing

I'VE BEEN HEAVY my whole life. In 8th grade, I was 200 pounds. Cristy talks about being an overweight athlete, and that's exactly what I was. In high school and college, I was a serious athlete. I got plenty of exercise, but it didn't help me lose weight. You can't outrun your fork.

At my heaviest weight, I was 298, right after my second miscarriage. The stress and depression from not being able to get pregnant was so hard. And then after losing the baby, my husband and I decided we just couldn't do this anymore. Something had to change.

My feet hurt as soon as I woke up; they didn't want to hold up my weight. My knees crunched. I felt fatigued and bloated. My joints were swollen, and I had frequent migraines. I ate convenience foods all the time. I'd stop and grab breakfast on my way to work and get a large coffee with a doughnut and a croissant. Then I'd run out for lunch and get a bagel with cream cheese. Then I'd come home to a decent dinner. But I ate like crap for most of the day.

At one point, I was exercising 12 times a week. I swam for an hour in the morning and took a spin class in the evening. I was determined to exercise off the weight, but I only lost 30 pounds. I felt great because of the endorphins, but it wasn't sustainable. I was trying to eat healthy. I ate fruit, vegetables, and protein—but we ate so much cheese and bread! I couldn't keep up all the exercise, so I gained the weight back.

Cool Whip, so technically it was okay. That just seems hilarious to me now! I think we all try to cheat the system however we can. On most plans, I could only lose like 15 or 20 pounds and never push

I have so much more energy. I wake up naturally in the morning and don't have to hit the snooze button 12 times. I don't get headaches nearly as often. The pain in my legs and my arms is completely gone. And I've had to get rid of about half the clothes in my closet! I'm wearing clothes in sizes that I haven't worn since high school.

I've tried so many ways to lose weight. Weight Watchers, pills, energy pills, compulsive exercising...nothing ever helped. Mainly because there are so many ways to cheat and still technically stay "on plan." Any program that stressed low-fat foods would allow things like low-fat yogurt and low-fat cheese sticks. I ate those a lot. My favorite "diet food" was Nutella and Cool Whip! Because you could get fat-free

past that. Now I know it's because I was eating the opposite of how I should eat.

THE EASIEST HARD THING YOU'LL EVER DO

My husband was actually the one who suggested we try Code Red. We had both tried to lose weight in the past, but could never get on board together at the

same time. This time was different. We were both ready to commit to a plan and support each other. We are in our early 30s—we shouldn't be feeling like crap or hating the way we look. It was the easiest hard thing we've ever done!

Cristy says you have to "pick your hard." Losing weight and changing your whole lifestyle is hard. No one is ever going to argue that. But being overweight is also hard. Waking up in pain is hard. Thinking about weight-loss surgery is hard. Code Red was the easiest hard thing we could do. I feel so full all the time. The whole plan feels sustainable—like we can do this forever.

My biggest surprise was how quickly and consistently the weight came off.

I set my first goal at 235. That's a weight I haven't seen in 8 years. I know I want to lose more than that, but I needed to feel successful. And that goal seemed like a stretch but not an impossible one. I have to say, I had lost a good 30 pounds before it finally hit me that I was doing it! This was actually working.

TALKING NICELY TO MYSELF

I love the instant feedback from weighing myself every day. If my weight stays the same or goes up a little bit, I know exactly why and I can correct it before it gets out of hand. Even if I stall for a few days, as long as I stick to the rules, the scale eventually starts moving in the right direction. A little while into this journey, I took a business trip across the country. I stuck to the program as much as I could, but my weight did go up about 5 pounds. As soon as I got back to the regular routine, it came right back off. No sweat!

It's interesting to me that the more often I talked nicely to myself and told myself it was okay to let the weight go, the faster the scale would move. Sometimes I would stall for 3 or 4 days and I'd have a little "staff meeting" with myself and say, "It's okay. You don't need to hold onto this weight." And then my weight would start to drop again.

We started March 18th. We couldn't start on the 17th because we wanted a beer for St. Patrick's Day. So we had a celebratory drink, and then started our new lifestyle. As of today, I'm 43 pounds down and I know I'm just going to keep losing.

I'm going to let my body decide when I should stop losing. I am 5'10", and I really don't know what my ideal weight will be. I mean, I've been over 200 pounds since 8th grade. But I trust my body now, and I'm a Rebel for life. So my body will figure out where it wants to settle in. If you had told me a few months ago that I could get below 200, I would have laughed so hard. But now, I don't know...it seems totally attainable on this plan.

YOU CAN'T CHEAT THE SYSTEM

The biggest tip I can give is to be honest with yourself. If you're just having a bite of ice cream or "just one beer", it shows up on the scale. Unlike other weight-loss programs, you can't cheat the system. You can't fake it. When you're honest

with yourself and you follow the rules, the weight comes off so naturally. It just does. You don't have to force it. You don't have to exercise compulsively. I think I've taken 3 walks in 4 months, and I've lost 43 pounds. It seems impossible, but I've seen it work.

The ripple effect has been amazing. We learned about the Code Red Lifestyle from my cousin. My father has been overweight most of his life and he decided to try it just to see if it would make a difference. And he's lost over 50 pounds. The man is a rockstar! He just had to uncover it. When I joined Cristy's 10-Pound Takedown challenge, people saw my progress and decided to join in. And they are all losing pounds as well. It's like we're the incredible shrinking family! And it's right, because we're worth

it. We deserve to live healthy lives without carrying all this extra weight.

Sometimes, I do get nervous about gaining the weight back. But the difference this time is that I have the tools to take it back off. I've already proven that I can do it. I've had weekends where I gained 5 pounds, but I was able to take it right back off and keep going.

I'm so incredibly blessed to have been put into the same sphere as Cristy. It's like the planets lined up and put her in my path or something. I've finally learned what we should have been taught growing up.

I am a Code Red Rebel, and I am so grateful for the changes I see in myself and my husband every day.

5 Let's Talk About Sugar

SUGAR IS HANDS DOWN THE BIGGEST cause of sickness, disease, and cancer in today's society. I know that's a bold statement, and a lot of people get defensive when I talk about it. It has been proven time and time again. It's poison at the levels we consume it today. There's a safe sugar threshold for humans, just like there's a safe threshold of anything—even arsenic.

Across the board, nutritionists agree that we should get no more than about 25 grams of sugar per day, which is roughly 6 teaspoons. Most people consume more than that within an hour of waking up. The average American gets about 150 grams of sugar per day, which is astonishing. That's just a mind-blowing amount of sugar.

The problem is we just don't realize how often we're consuming it. Okay, yeah, that morning doughnut has sugar. That's easy to spot. But what about the healthy salad you're eating for lunch? The one with the dried cranberries (26g of sugar in ⅓ cup) and the low-fat dressing? Food doesn't have to taste sweet to have added sugar.

In fact, as you consume more sugar, your taste buds become numb to sweetness. You have to add more and more sugar to get the same sensation of

69

sweetness. Once you remove sugar from your diet, your taste buds return to normal, and foods you used to love will suddenly be too sickly sweet to eat.

If you want to dive deep into the science behind sugar and its unholy alliance with the manufactured food industry, I highly recommend reading *Salt, Sugar, Fat* and watching the documentary *Fed Up*. But let's put all that aside for now and just focus on the affect sugar has on your weight.

Remember that your body can run on glucose or ketones. Glucose is sugar. So naturally, the more sugar you consume, the more energy your body has available. Of course, we consume *way* more than we need, so it all gets stored away as fat. Once again, your body is just doing its job—saving up for when there's no food available.

The Code Red answer to this is pretty obvious—don't eat sugar or foods that easily break down into sugar, such as bread, pasta, or alcohol. If you're trying to burn excess fat by converting it to ketones, you can't be adding sugar to the equation.

But that is easier said than done, right? Sugar is everywhere!

Here's What Sugar Does Inside Your Body

We're going to keep this simple, okay? When you eat sugar or any simple carbohydrates that turn into sugar—such as bread, cereal, pasta, or rice—your blood sugar level immediately spikes. The liver can only store a small amount of glucose (sugar) for immediate use. So the excess stays in the bloodstream. In a healthy person, the pancreas then secretes insulin to bring those blood sugar levels back down so you don't die. Insulin is a vital hormone. It helps the body store that extra sugar as fat, so we can access it later.

It's a beautiful system. The problem is that our modern society and "normal" eating habits have made it so we eat massive doses of sugar or glucose-producing foods. Because of that, we have to release massive doses of insulin, and we store huge amounts of fat for later. The problem is that "later" never comes. We aren't living in caves as hunters and gatherers anymore. We have plenty of food. We may never need to use up all that stored fat.

While this amazing process is happening in your body, you will feel great for a few minutes when your liver is filling up with glucose. This is that "sugar high" you get after eating a doughnut or a big plate of pasta. But then what happens? You know the answer. You get a sugar crash, right? Your energy tanks, and you might even feel a little light-headed or sick. And then what happens? You crave more sugar to get you back up to that high again. Your body is screaming at you to eat more sugar!

Remember, this is a survival mechanism. Your body is trying to keep you alive! So trying to resist those cravings is next to impossible over the long term. The best thing you can do is avoid them altogether. Can you imagine a life where you have no cravings for sugary sweets or desserts? It is totally possible! When you eat a high-fat diet regularly, there are no spikes. There are no crashes. And there are no physical cravings.

It's really not hard to keep your sugar intake down, once you become aware of how much sugar is in everything. So the food industry has gotten really tricky. They've figured out how to call sugar other names to fool you—61 other names, to be exact. If you see words like these on your food labels, you're looking at sugar: brown sugar, cane crystals, cane sugar, corn sweetener, corn syrup, corn syrup solids, crystal dextrose, dextrose, evaporated cane juice, fructose sweetener, or fruit juice.

Sugar is cheap and it makes manufactured foods taste better—so they add tons of it to just about everything you consume.

Here's the dirty little secret about sugar: it's addictive. The more you eat it, the more you crave it. It's been proven to be 8 times more addictive than cocaine. That's not a number I just made up. It's actually been measured and proven! Can you imagine how hard it would be to just "unplug" from cocaine or heroin using pure willpower? It would be just about impossible, especially if it was just lying around your home and you were expected to use it multiple times a day. Could anyone ever detox from drugs if they were advertised to them 24/7? Of course not!

We demonize and vilify addictive drugs like cocaine, heroin, and even tobacco. But sugar isn't classified as a drug, even though it's just as addictive and causes horrible health problems. Sugar is celebrated in this country. In fact, it seems to be a required component of any celebration we hold—from birthdays to weddings to holidays. It's added to just about every manufactured food available. It's marketed to children through cartoons and video games. Unless you live under a rock, it's practically impossible to escape the influence of sugar. It's not your fault that you're addicted to it—you're simply part of a massive marketing campaign designed to make a few companies extremely wealthy.

So what can you do about it?

Your first task is to be honest with yourself. How much sugar do you really consume every day? My guess is that it's way more than you think! With awareness comes power. Once you're aware of what's happening, you can start to do something about it. The only way to really know how much sugar you consume each day is to track your food intake. I know that doesn't sound like much fun, but it's critical to your success. You've got to track your food for at least a little while to find out where your sugar's coming from and where you need to improve. What foods do you need to cut out? What foods do you need to add in? I can throw a bunch of numbers at you, but that's not going to mean anything until you actually start tracking.

I use a great app with my clients called Lose It. Start by downloading the app on your phone, or just get a notebook and start writing down everything you eat during the course of a day. Specifically, **WRITE DOWN EXACTLY WHAT YOU'RE EATING AND HOW MUCH**. Don't guess. Get a nutrition chart and a food scale and weigh it. Even just tracking the calorie and sugar content of your food will be a good start. Enter everything into the app, and you will get a great snapshot of what you're eating each day.

Track your food for a week, and I guarantee you will be shocked by what you discover. Even when you're eating "healthy," you're probably going to find yourself way over that recommended 25g of sugar.

But what about natural sugars? Those don't count, do they?

It all counts!

Added sugars are easy to spot. If you're eating anything in a box or a wrapper, it's probably got added sugar. But fruits and vegetables have natural sugars. Honey and maple syrup are natural sugars. It all counts toward that 25g limit.

PARTY SURVIVAL GUIDE

You're cruising along through the week. Drinking your water. Keeping track of your sugar. When **BAM!** Friday hits. Party time! How do you keep from completely blowing all your progress in 24 hours? Here are some quick strategies to help you keep calm and party on.

Food

- Eat before you go. Don't head out the door hungry.

- Mingle. Don't stand by the snack table.

- Chew gum. Lots of gum. (It's rude to blow bubbles in your boss's face, though.)

- Keep a glass of water in your hand and sip on it all night.

- Wear something tight and sexy. Loose clothing can make you a little too comfortable and more likely to pig out.

- If you must eat something, go for the veggies and dip. (Or better yet, just the veggies.) Dip may load you up with calories, but it won't do as much damage as cookies and cake.

- Choose the smallest plate possible, eat slowly, and avoid seconds.

Which means if you're in weight-loss mode, you're going to want to avoid all natural sugars, too. That means no fruits or starchy vegetables like potatoes.

Now, naturally occurring sugars also come with amazing vitamins, minerals, and other healthy substances our bodies need. So you don't want to be stuck in weight-loss mode forever. Once you're at your goal weight, you can safely add in a serving of fruit here and there. My goal is to help you get the weight off as quickly as possible. And to do that, you're going to have to cut out most fruits. The

Drink

- If you're drinking alcohol, stick to clear varieties like gin or vodka.

- Mix with diet tonic or diet Sprite (not a sugary juice).

- Avoid the beer—it's too high in calories.

- Choose red wine—it's got fewer calories than white or blush.

- Stick to one and done—have one drink and that's it (especially if you're driving).

- Plan on going to the gym or an early run (to encourage an earlier bedtime).

Try being the photographer at the party—it will keep your hands and mind busy and away from the snack table. Laugh, dance, play games, run around after the kids—enjoy your party! The laughter is the best part, and it's calorie-free.

good news is that berries like strawberries and blueberries are low-sugar. So they can be eaten during weight-loss mode. Just don't overdo it. Track everything.

No one is going to police your sugar consumption for you. In fact, manufacturers are going to do their best to get you to consume as much as possible. So if it has a package, a box, or a wrapper, check the label for sugar content. Or better yet, just don't eat it at all. The less you eat out of packages, the better.

What About Artificial Sweeteners?

Here's a tricky subject: Is it okay to substitute artificial sweeteners when you're cutting out sugar? The answer is that it depends. You have to pay very close attention to what happens with your weight when you consume different types and different amounts of this stuff. Different people have different tolerances. You might be able to use sucralose (Splenda) or stevia—or you might find your weight loss stalls when you use it. Some people tolerate erythritol (sugar alcohol) just fine, and others wind up with diarrhea.

The problem, according to some studies, seems to be that if our brain even senses sweetness, meaning we taste something sweet, it initiates an insulin response in our bodies. So even though the chemical sweetener itself technically shouldn't affect us the same as sugar, in reality it does.

Besides releasing insulin, which tells the body to store fat, that sweet taste can also trigger cravings. Once we taste something sweet, we naturally want more of it. Because, to your body, storing fat means you're more likely to survive the hard, cold winter when food is scarce. So even "safe" sweeteners can wind up causing us to overeat. But again, this doesn't happen for everyone.

It's your job to keep track of how much artificial sweetener you're using and notice what's happening with your body. Are your sugar cravings worse? Are you moody and irritable? Is your weight loss stalled? Keeping track and maintaining 100% honesty are the keys to figuring out your body's response to all types of sweeteners.

Rodger Williams

Pushed Through Trauma and Anxiety and Lost 72 Pounds (So Far!)

BEFORE 2011, I thought I was doing okay with my health. Then my roommate and best friend died in a tragic accident. That's when all my health issues started to crop up. I still have a hard time even thinking about it. Like most people, I guess I used food and alcohol to sort of numb my feelings, and my weight just kept going up and up. I was completely addicted to Reese's peanut butter cups.

Eventually, I did manage to give up drinking, and was rewarded with gout and a celiac diagnosis. To make matters worse, I suffered extreme anxiety to the point where I couldn't go to work, shop for groceries, or even leave the house. Until recently, I had only left my little town twice in five years.

I had tried to lose weight in the past, but nothing ever worked. I bought a treadmill and a stepper, but after a couple of days, I just stopped using them.

A REASON TO TRY

Then earlier this year, I found out my daughter was pregnant. And I felt it was finally time to lose the weight so I could be there for her and the baby. Even though I had made up my mind, I didn't really know what to do until I saw Ryan Smathers' post about Code Red on his Facebook feed. We

MARCH 1ST
MARCH 1ST
JULY 10TH
JULY 10TH

were friends, and I thought if he could do it, then I could do it.

At that point, I weighed 277 pounds. The results Cristy was talking about sounded too good to be true. But I trusted Ryan, and I figured $37 for 6 weeks of coaching wasn't too much of a risk. So I signed up for the 10-Pound Takedown challenge. And my life hasn't been the same since.

I came up with all the reasons this program wouldn't work. I thought my anxiety would get in the way, or the celiac. I'm a night owl. I'm a couch potato. And I knew I was a really picky eater—I hate berries, yogurt, and most veggies. But the Code Red community believed in me. They cheered me on right from the start, and wouldn't let me quit on myself. I had always given up on weight loss before because there was no one there to really care whether I succeeded or not. Now I have friends cheering me on, and I get to show them support, too.

IT'S NOT JUST ABOUT THE WEIGHT LOSS

You learn to deal with anxiety by creating routines for yourself, like what times you eat. That concerned me because of the 6:30 rule. But I figured it was a small price to pay for losing the weight. My anxiety was so bad, I had a routine for going to the grocery store. I had to plan what I was getting ahead of time, know where it was all located, rehearse it a few times in my head, and then go to the store and just get those things and leave. I only went to one store a few blocks away.

Recently, I realized I don't need a set plan to go to the store anymore. I can now go to other places, like Albertsons. And while I still plan it out, I can deviate from the list and go look for other things if I think of something I want. In the past, I would just leave without looking for that extra item because staying would lead to panic attacks. Before I started living the Code

Red Lifestyle, I couldn't go anywhere. I've been dealing with this crippling anxiety for over 6 years, without drugs. And now after a few short months, I finally feel like I might actually be completely free of it someday.

OF COURSE, THE WEIGHT LOSS IS GREAT TOO!

I started drinking water before the challenge officially started and lost 7 pounds, even though I wasn't following the rules yet. Then the challenge started and I had to follow the rules. The first time I stepped on the scale after I stopped eating all the crap, I had lost 6.6 pounds in one day! I was just flabbergasted. I had no idea I could eat food that I liked and

actually lose weight. I had to go back and weigh myself like four times because I couldn't believe the number. After the third day, I started to think, "Hey, I can do this." And I fell into the routine of working the program. It's still a pattern, but it's a much healthier pattern.

I think I lost 16 pounds in the first week to 10 days, and then there was no turning back. I was so relieved that I found something that was going to work. I just followed the rules and stayed connected to Cristy throughout the challenge. I didn't have the money to invest in a private program, so I just keep trucking along on my own. And I keep losing weight.

The biggest surprise to me was how easy the plan is. I still get to eat all the foods

I love, and I'm coming out of my shell a little to try cooking more. My mom reads women's magazines, and there's a new diet every week. I would glance at them

I used to have a lot of skin problems from the celiac disease, but that's all gone now. The chronic dandruff has gone away. My gout has been held in check. It's a life-

I came up with all the reasons this program wouldn't work. I thought my anxiety would get in the way, or the celiac. I'm a night owl. I'm a couch potato. And I knew I was a really picky eater.

and go, "Yuck! I could never do that...the shakes and pills and things. No way!"

I'm at 205 now, and I'm still losing. In the beginning of April, I was able to go to Walmart for the first time in 5 years. And I was able to attend my daughter's ultrasound, which is the first time I'd ventured out of my hometown in years. I'm really proud of myself.

changer because I can actually go out and do stuff. I can have a life again. I'm hoping I can attend the birth of my grandson. I'm not really concerned about gaining the weight back. The food is too good, and I feel amazing. There's no way I would go back now.

Thank you, Cristy, for giving me my life back!

6 Fat Fills You Up

FAT MAKES FOOD TASTE GOOD. It is satisfying. It fills us up. We need fat to survive. Yet we get confused about it because it's the same stuff hanging off our tummies and our butts that we're trying so hard to get rid of.

Let's clear this up right now. There's body fat and dietary fat. The fat on your body—the stuff you want to lose—that's nothing more than stored-up energy. When your body runs out of primary fuel, it will start using that stored fuel. The problem is that our bodies never run out of primary fuel. So we remain overweight.

When we refer to "fat" as a nutrient, or dietary fat, we're looking at an amazing substance. You can't live without it. Fat helps your hair and nails grow. It assists in normal brain development, and helps you absorb vitamins A, D, E, and K. You can get fat from animal products like chicken, bacon, and steak. And you can also get healthy fat from plant sources like avocados, coconut oil, olive oil, nuts, and seeds.

Government guidelines since 1977 have recommended that Americans reduce the amount of fat in their diets to avoid the risk of stroke, heart disease, and other problems. In response to the low-fat call to arms, the food industry stepped up to produce hundreds of thousands of products that they market as "healthy" and "fat-free," yet are totally devoid of nutrition. We shovel fistfuls of fat-free snacks into our mouths, not realizing we are just making ourselves fatter and less healthy.

The fat-free craze that has taken over our society is a major cause of our obesity epidemic. When the food industry had to take the fat out of processed foods, they added sugar and carbs back in to make it taste good. Technically, a bag of pure cane sugar could legally display the label "fat-free." It is. There's no fat in there. But that label would be incredibly misleading, because people have been taught to think that fat-free means healthy. It doesn't. Consuming that product would make you fat, even though it contains no dietary fat.

Food labels are more about advertising than health. That same bag of sugar can also claim it's "gluten-free" and even "all-natural" under the right circum-stances. That doesn't mean it's healthy. Don't pay attention to the front of the package. Pay attention to the label on the back or the side. Read the actual ingredients. The fewer the ingredients, the better. Keep the artificial chemicals to a minimum, and avoid sugar whenever you can.

Contrary to what the government or your well-meaning neighbors might say, lowering your fat intake will not make any difference in your weight loss. The right fats—like avocados, olives, and naturally occurring oils such as olive and coconut—can actually aid weight loss. (As long as you're very careful with the calorie content of those fats.)

Dietary fat doesn't make you fat.

Sugar makes you fat. Because it's excess energy being stored away.

HEALTHY FATS

FATS TO EAT	FATS TO AVOID
👍 Avocados	👎 Canola oil
👍 Bacon	👎 Corn oil
👍 Beef Tallow	👎 Cottonseed oil
👍 Butter	👎 Hydrogenated oils
👍 Coconut Oil	👎 Peanut oil
👍 Eggs (with yolk)	👎 Margarine
👍 Flaxseed oil	👎 Mayonnaise containing the listed oils
👍 Ghee	👎 Safflower oil
👍 Heavy cream, whipping cream, half-and-half	👎 Soybean oil
👍 Lard	
👍 Nuts and nut butters (except peanuts)	
👍 Olive oil	
👍 Olives	
👍 Palm oil	
👍 Pork fat	
👍 Seafood (herring, salmon, sardines, tuna)	
👍 Sour cream	

Control how much sugar and simple carbohydrates you're consuming, and you'll be well on your way to that weight loss and healthy lifestyle you desire.

We're going to talk more about fat later on. For now, let's make it easy on you. If it says "fat-free" on the front label, put it down. Don't eat it. Seriously, you're better off eating the full-fat version, if you eat it at all.

Stacey Hylen

Lost 50 Pounds Without Being Hungry

I'VE BEEN ACTIVE my whole life. And even though I was working out every day, I didn't have a lot of energy. I just figured that was normal. These days, I'm always running around. I have a business, two kids at home, and one of my daughters is a national-level competitive gymnast. My whole schedule runs around her—taking her to massage, to physio, and to the gym for training. And she's had a broken back recently, so I had a lot of stress around her health. When I'm stressed, I eat!

Even though I've worked out every day since I was 14, I was still heavy because I was *always* hungry. I would eat and eat, and my mom would say, "You're not starving!" And I'd say, "Yes, I am! **I'M STARVING TO DEATH!**"

When I was in high school, I did a term paper on fake fats like olestra. And my ex was a body builder. So I knew a thing or two about nutrition, or so I thought. I ate very low-fat, which was what we were

told was the right thing to do. I was so miserable. I would eat healthy Monday through Friday, and then have some treats on the weekend. But I just ate all the time.

A while ago, my kids asked me how I gained the weight in the first place. And I had to think about it. I realized that I was so stressed and tired from being a new mom and running my business that I would eat to wake up. I ate convenience food. And I ate low-fat. I got my energy from foods, which would have been fine except I was getting sugar spikes and crashes from eating the wrong food.

I was at the point where I had resigned myself to being curvy and "voluptuous"

forever. My highest weight was 198, and I could get down to 180 or 175. But I could never break through that barrier. Most of the programs I tried took so long. Losing one pound a week is just depressing. It feels like you'll *never* reach your goal, even if you do everything right. I would eat bland broiled chicken breast and veggies and quinoa all the time, and lose like a half a pound. Then I'd gain it all back on the weekend. It was an awful cycle.

Then I saw my friend Natasha at an event, and she had lost so much weight with Code Red in just a few months. It was amazing to see. We are sort of the same body type, and at events people often think we're sisters. It gave me some hope that maybe I could do this thing, too. But I wasn't willing to do anything crazy like weird pills or hormones or whatever. (I was a little nervous that that's what this was all about.) But I decided to try it.

Then along comes Cristy telling me to sleep and manage my stress and eat exactly backward from what I thought was healthy...and it worked. I couldn't believe how well it worked. I was not a fast loser. I was actually weight-loss resistant. But this was something I could stick to forever. I didn't want the junk anymore. And I wasn't thinking in terms of "Oh!

The 12-week program is over. I can go back to eating normally now." I actually wanted to keep eating this way.

THE MINDSET SHIFT

I went to Arizona for 10 days and my mom made cookies and brownies and things. But I stuck to the program the whole time. Then I turned around and went to Hawaii for 10 days on a cruise. And the only non-approved items I had were 2 dark chocolate macadamia nuts and 1 bite of pineapple. Seriously, that was my "cheat"—2 nuts and a bite of fruit! I was completely satisfied with my filet

I needed to invest in myself and I needed someone who would not let me quit on myself. And that's Cristy. She believed in me fiercely, and wouldn't take my lame excuses for why I wasn't making progress.

When I started working with Cristy, and I completely flipped everything and started eating high-fat—it was like a miracle. For the first time, I wasn't hungry! I started to think I could actually do this.

mingon and veggies. I was happy with my food. I didn't need a french fry to make me happy. That was a huge mindset shift for me. And that was when I knew this was going to work, and it was for life.

My husband has also lost weight, even though he didn't need to. It's just happening as a side effect of living with me. My kids have been so influenced by Cristy. We're watching documentaries and cooking shows together. We're reading labels together. They are deciding for themselves that they want to eat healthier. All my kids are eating a lot less sugar. They are really young and fit, but just from being exposed to the Code Red Lifestyle, they naturally want to eat better. This is definitely how I'm living the rest of my life. I don't ever want to go back to where I was.

If you're not sure about starting this lifestyle, read all these success stories. We are all people just like you. We all have kids and work challenges and life stress. And we all made it work. And you can, too.

7 The Truth About Gluten

I JUST TOLD YOU ABOUT THE 1970S, 80S, AND 90S, when everyone blamed dietary fat for all their problems. The food industry went wild marketing low-fat everything. Well, gluten is the new fat. It's poorly understood, and it seems like everyone has an opinion about it. It's been demonized to the point where everyone thinks it's the root of all their problems. Funnily enough, the average person can't even tell you what gluten is.

Gluten is a protein found in wheat and other grains. Nothing more.

People who have been properly diagnosed and know they suffer from celiac disease need to avoid gluten entirely. Celiac is a serious autoimmune disease in which gluten severely damages a person's small intestine. Their bodies react badly to it. It is also hereditary, so a person with celiac disease has a 1 in 10 chance of passing it to their kids. Gluten is a very real problem for these folks. Some people are gluten-intolerant, which means their bodies don't make the enzyme to break gluten down. These people also need to be careful around the stuff.

For the rest of the world, though, gluten is probably the healthiest part of the wheat grain. It's just a protein. The diet industry has brainwashed you into believing it's the enemy, but it's not. The problems people blame on gluten are more often the result of the actual grains themselves. The aching joints, belly fat, fatigue—that all comes from consuming too many starchy carbs and sugar in your diet, not from gluten.

It would be laughable if it weren't so sad. People spend their hard-earned money on gluten-free breads and crackers believing they are getting healthier, yet nothing changes! That's because it's still bread, folks. It's still crackers.

The simple carbohydrates that convert into sugar are all still there.

For the average adult, gluten is not a problem. Unless your doctor has diagnosed you with celiac or has told you that you can't produce the enzyme for digesting gluten, your problems are the result of too many carbs in your diet. You're better off just avoiding bread altogether than buying the expensive gluten-free variety. Get rid of the carbs and sugar and you'll feel better.

The same is often true of lactose. Most Americans can process lactose just fine. Some of my clients used to think they were lactose intolerant, but later found out it wasn't the lactose that was bothering them. The sugar and the carbs in the dairy products were the problems.

The food industry wants people to get in on the gluten-free fad. They get to sell the same products with the gluten stripped out. And guess what? People keep buying their products because they're still packed with sugar and carbs and they taste good.

So if you think you are gluten-sensitive or gluten-intolerant, get checked out by your doctor. I mean, actually **SEE YOUR DOCTOR AND GET A DIAGNOSIS**. Internet research doesn't count. Chances are, gluten is not your problem.

Once you retrain your body to burn fat instead of sugar, you will see a lot of those problems disappear.

Once again, we're talking about reaching a weight-loss goal here. It's not like you can't have pizza or a sandwich for the rest of your life. When you get down to your goal weight, you will be able to have an occasional English muffin without any inflammation or stomach upset. I call it the 90/10 rule. You eat right 90% of the time and stray a little bit 10% of the time. Even folks who have irritable bowel syndrome (IBS) find that issue can be fixed by nutrition.

About 17 years ago, I suffered from IBS so badly that I was on medication for it. I was intimately familiar with that fear of eating anything that might trigger those agonizing sharp pains. I was afraid to engage in any activity that might trigger an attack. And I couldn't stray too far from a bathroom. It was awful.

Once I started eating by the Code Red rules and cut out all grains, sugars, and simple carbs, it was 100% cured. Seriously, when I stopped eating inflammatory foods, the symptoms just disappeared and I stopped taking all that medication. These days, my body is healthy and there's little or no inflammation. So I can eat the occasional piece of pizza or sugary treat and not suffer any ill effects. But if I were to disregard the rules regularly, the inflammation would return and I'd suffer those painful episodes all over again. No thanks!

Real, wholesome, natural food will not irritate a healthy digestive system.

Here's the good news: None of the foods you eat with the Code Red Lifestyle have gluten in them.

No grains, no wheat, no gluten.

No problem.

Brian Caldwell

Lost 35 Pounds and Has Kept it Off For 2 Years

I'VE BEEN an active person my whole life. Whether it was running, cycling, swimming, or weight training, I have been a fit, athletic person for as long as I can remember. However, as I approached middle-age, I did notice my weight start to creep up on me. At first I chalked it up to age, but over the course of 10 years or so, it reached a point that I just wasn't happy with. My life was out of balance. I was working close to 80 hours a week. I stayed as active as I could, given those

hours, but that much work forced me into a more sedentary lifestyle.

I was eating like someone 10 or 15 years younger, and I just couldn't keep up with the pace of my life at that time. I wasn't grossly overweight, but it had reached a point where it was affecting all aspects of my life.

Fortunately, my wife heard about Cristy from a mutual friend, and we decided to meet with her. Like I said, I have been fitness-minded my entire life, so I did not need as much lifestyle correction as some people might. Still, there were some highly valuable tools and information that my wife and I both took away from our time with Cristy.

For one, I had no idea how dehydrated I was. I mean, I drank plenty throughout the day, but it was not nearly as much water as Cristy recommends people drink. Honestly, drinking a gallon or so of water every day was the biggest adjustment for me. Again, I wasn't in the habit of eating junk food, so I didn't have to go through a major detox period.

All in all, Cristy's program made a lot of sense to me. For the longest time, I had avoided fats. And I didn't know the dangers those simple carbohydrates posed. The commonly accepted literature

in this country tells people to avoid fats, and everyone has heard of athletes and carb-loading. Cristy's program definitely educated me about sugar.

I weighed about 215 pounds to start, when my wife and I signed up for a 30-day program with Cristy. Over the course of about 90 days, I lost 35 pounds. I will say, it is an intense program. Cristy is very thorough in her attention to her clients.

What I really appreciate is that she gives you the tools to continue on your own. Fortunately, my wife and I both adopted the mindset that we were going to do this and stick to it, so we did not need too much in the way of oversight from Cristy. For us, it was more about learning

I feel like I got to reset to where my life was 10 years ago. I feel rejuvenated. My activity level is back up to what it was when I was younger. My mindset is healthier than it was. I found out what I had to do to get the extra weight off, and I feel like I have restored balance to my life.

I feel like I got to reset to where my life was 10 years ago.

what we had to do to reach our goals, and Cristy is very good at that. She has simple rules, and gives procedures that are easy to follow.

You do what she says; you lose weight.

So my wife and I both reached our targets, and we have kept the weight off for 2 years. Again, because Cristy has given us the tools to maintain healthy weights, we're not concerned about gaining any of it back, and that is the most valuable aspect of the program from my point of view.

My advice to you, if you're considering the Code Red Lifestyle, is to be mentally ready to take it on. Don't sign up to "give it a try" or "give it a shot." If you are ready to make a change in your life, *you* have to establish your mindset to commit, because ultimately you are the one in control. Cristy will tell you what to do and what to change, but *you* have to be the one to do it.

If you want to work with Cristy and change your life, commit 100%!

8 The Deal with Dairy

LET'S TALK MILK. Did you know we are the only species that drinks another species' milk? In addition, we are the only species that continues to drink milk after we've been weaned. These are some of the reasons I am not a big fan of milk.

I stopped drinking milk about 10 years ago and, except for the heavy cream I put in my coffee, I consume very little dairy. People weren't meant to drink milk throughout their lives, but some people do.

So what's the deal with milk? Most parents give their kids milk. After all, "It does a body good," right? If you're going to give your kids milk, at least bite the bullet and give them whole milk. Studies show that one glass of whole milk is equal to two glasses of skim, or even 1% or 2% milk. Skim milk has had most or all of the fat removed. What happens when you take all the fat out of something? It tastes awful. If you give kids skim milk, they're just going to ask for chocolate or strawberry syrup to make it taste better. Give them whole milk if they must have milk.

The fact is, we as a society have been brainwashed over the past 40 years into thinking we need to drink milk. "You need milk to get your calcium." Bullcrap.

You get more calcium from spinach and chia seeds than you could ever get from milk. Some research indicates that milk actually leaches calcium from your bones, not the other way around. I prefer whipping cream in my coffee, if I am going to have dairy. However, when I need to lose some weight for a photo shoot or something, the dairy is the first thing to go.

If you must have dairy in your coffee, I really do recommend heavy cream. Even for you folks using half-and-half—the heavy cream is more calorie-dense, but you need so much less of it to cream up your coffee. Dairy is not going to spike your blood sugar, unless it's ice cream or something with a ton of sugar added. But it will prevent you from losing weight. I urge my clients to drop the dairy while they're losing weight.

But...but...cheese!

As long as we're being honest, let's consider cheese for a minute. It's got no sugar and no carbs, and it's a great source of fat. So we ought to be able to roll around in a huge tub of Brie with no regrets, right?

Theoretically, yes. but cheese is extremely calorie-dense. That means there are a lot of calories packed into one little ounce of the stuff. (One ounce is roughly 100 grams, for you metric folks.)

Different cheeses have different calorie counts, but in general one ounce of hard cheese is 110 calories. There's really no way to know what one ounce actually is unless you slice it and weigh it. So one day I did that. I sliced it, I weighed it, and I found out that it's not very big at all. You could easily go back for a second, third, fourth, or fifth slice of cheese. Heck, it's easy to polish off half a block without even thinking about it. Pretty soon, you've packed on 500 to 1,000 extra calories, and you have no idea why you're gaining weight.

And hey, when cheese is melted all ooey-gooey in a spinach dip or on a pizza, who knows exactly how much you're eating. It's really hard to tell!

It could just be the math that's been keeping you fat.

Be honest with yourself, that's all I ask.

Now, some dairy foods can be tolerated in weight-loss mode without showing up on the scale. Sour cream, cream cheese, cottage cheese, and heavy cream are all okay if you consume the full-fat variety. Just be very careful to measure and log how much you're eating, so there are no surprises.

Tara Rowland

Lost 105 Pounds and Renewed Her Family

LET ME START by saying that I have been heavy pretty much my entire life, at least since 2nd or 3rd grade. As an adult, I tried just about every weight-loss program, diet, or gimmick that's out there: Richard Simmons' "Move, Groove and Lose" program, Weight Watchers, Prism, South Beach, Body By Vi, and Valosity, and I had been to a dietician. *Everything*. I was even moderately successful on some of them. I could always lose about 20 or 25 pounds, but never as much as I really needed to. When I did manage to lose weight, I always gained it back, usually with a little extra. So I know what it's like to be heavy, because I did it for the first 30 years of my life. I know what it is like to try many different things that are supposed to work, but just don't.

Finally, I reached a point with my weight where I just didn't care anymore. I ate whatever, I quit exercising. Nothing I tried seemed to work anyway. In addition to that, my family had moved, and I think I was dealing with some depression.

I HAD GIVEN UP ON MY BODY

Now, I have known Cristy my whole life. Our grandmothers were sisters. For the past year and a half, I had been watching what she was doing on Facebook. I saw all

and I thought I was going to have to call someone to come pick me up.

I did manage to finish, but that moment in the 5K was my rock-bottom moment. I truly did not know whether I was going to fail in front of my kids and my community. That feeling of dread, on top of my exhaustion, is one I will never forget. To make matters worse, I saw pictures of myself afterward, and I just couldn't believe how heavy and unhealthy I had become. I almost didn't recognize myself.

That was my deciding moment. I took a shower and then drove an hour to the women's event to meet up with Cristy.

the success stories, and I ended up being invited to a women's conference that she held in a nearby town. But I decided I wasn't going to go.

That day, I participated in a community Fun Run that my three daughters wanted to do as part of our 4-H Making the Most of Me group. It was a 5K and I had never done anything like it before, but my girls were really excited about it. So I decided to do it with them. About half-way through, I had serious doubts as to whether I would finish. I was absolutely miserable. It was humiliating. All our friends were there, my kids were there,

After her presentation, she came over to say hello, and I just burst into tears. I asked her, "How do I fix my brain?" I had lost weight before. I knew what healthy was. I just didn't know how to get my brain to stop craving food all the time. Cristy was wonderful. She gave me a big hug, told me it wasn't my fault, and said, "I can help you."

I took some of the tools she shared in that August conference, and I worked on those on my own until January. Just doing that, I managed to lose about 20–25 pounds on my own. I was really frustrated through the holidays though, because I just had so much weight to lose. I wasn't sure I could do it alone.

At that point, I decided to call Cristy and talk to her about a one-on-one program. As a mother, it can be hard to spend money on yourself, but I made the decision with Cristy to invest the money and really stick with the program. My husband was very supportive, and my family in general were all behind me and wanted me to make a positive change for myself.

Once I began the process, coming off sugar was a miserable, terrible time. The most difficult part for me was reprogramming my brain to see food as fuel instead of a reward, stress reliever, comforter,

When I was growing up, everything we did revolved around food. Both of my grandmothers, as well as my mom, were

I just didn't know how to get my brain to stop craving food all the time. Cristy was wonderful. She gave me a big hug, told me it wasn't my fault, and said, "I can help you."

or gift. I quickly realized that food is an addiction like any other. I feel like I still do battle with my food-brain almost every day.

phenomenal cooks and the family get-togethers all centered around food. Trying to be with family for gatherings without eating was difficult because it was such a habit to eat and because I felt bad about what my family was eating. I was learning this new lifestyle, but they were not.

You might change, but the world around you doesn't. And all those cakes and sweets and delicious foods are still there. The grocery store is the worst; there's junk food wherever you turn. I still catch myself thinking that I should buy some little treat or reward for my kids. That being said, the changes in my food choices were really not all that difficult. I can go out to eat with friends at almost any restaurant and find something that fits into my plan.

The difference between the Code Red Lifestyle and all the other diets that I tried is in the name...it's a lifestyle. I eat normal food and I'm never hungry. But I also needed some of Cristy's tough love from time to time. I needed the accountability and the support. I needed to spend the money, because I was not about to mess up and flush all that money down the toilet. I needed to really pay attention to what I was eating and how I viewed food so I could make a real change. A lot of that came in conversations with Cristy. I was actually able to change my brain!

When I started, I weighed 275 pounds. I began changing my lifestyle in August

of 2015, and was down to 255 by January 2016, when I started working one-on-one with Cristy. I finally reached my first goal of 200 pounds in August 2016. I did another one-on-one program with Cristy in January of 2017, and have since lost another 30 pounds, so I am right around 170 now. I haven't reached my goal weight yet, but I'm confident that I will.

THE DIFFERENCE I FEEL IS ALMOST INDESCRIBABLE

I think back to that 5K I almost didn't finish, and realize that I was a completely different person then. I don't suffer in the heat anymore. I used to just sit in the house in the air-conditioning, but now I am outdoors with my girls, and I actually

enjoy warm weather. Before I lost the weight, I was told that I was pre-diabetic; that's no longer the case. I couldn't wear my wedding ring for years because it was too small; now I can't wear it because it's too big.

I used to wear a size 28, and I had to order a lot of my clothing from a catalogue or specialty stores. I wear a size 11/12 now, and I can buy clothes from any regular store. Unless you've been heavy like I was, you don't know what that is like. I went into a Victoria's Secret and bought a bra there for the first time. I cried right there in the store—tears of pure joy. I never imagined I'd be able to do that.

My family has become much more active too. My husband and girls are so supportive and perfectly content to eat the way I am eating because it is all real food. But the way we spend time together is different now. When we go on vacations, the focus is less on what we're eating, and more on what we're *doing*. Instead of, "Well, what restaurant should we go to?" It's "Where's a good hiking trail or park we can go to?" As a family, we walked 400 miles last summer to raise money for our school track project, and we're working on another 200 this year.

As a mother, I love knowing that I am teaching my daughters how to have a healthy relationship with food and that I can prevent them from struggling with their weight and bad health by breaking the cycle. Food is fuel...period.

STICKING WITH THE PROGRAM

If I could give any advice to people interested in making this change in their lives, it would be to just stick with it. Losing weight the right way involves changing your life, so it will not happen magically overnight. Sure, it happens fast in the beginning, but when the progress on the scale begins to slow down, or if you face a setback of any kind, my advice is to just stick with it. In my case, it took me 30 years to get as heavy as I did. And 30 years of an unhealthy lifestyle doesn't just disappear in the blink of an eye. I have lost over 100 pounds, but it's taken me more than a year and a half to do it. I even took a couple of breaks during that time, but I stayed true to the program.

There will be times when the scale doesn't show progress. That happened to me recently. You know what I did? I had my husband take my measurements. It turned out that I had lost a full 60 inches throughout my entire body! So even when the scale isn't moving, your body is still changing for the better.

Stick with it.

Even if you get stalled or sidetracked, don't ever give up. And be prepared to cry a lot of tears on this journey. I know I did. I cried frustrated tears, sad tears, mad tears, but more than any of those, I cried happy tears. I keep that picture of me from that 5K I almost didn't finish, as a reminder of what I have accomplished. And when people ask me, "What *diet* are you on now?" I reply, "It's the last one!"

9 Controversial Weight-Loss Methods

I'M GUESSING YOU'VE TRIED TO LOSE WEIGHT IN THE PAST. You probably saw some amazing advertising on TV or in a magazine and wanted what they were promising. Am I right? And since you're here reading this, you probably gained that weight right back (if you lost anything at all).

Here's the deal. All the popular weight-loss methods have something in common. The pills, the shakes, the weird diet foods, the extreme exercise programs—they're all just quick fixes.

They're gimmicks.

A gimmick isn't going to heal your life. Can they help you lose weight? Sure, maybe. Will you drink canned shakes for the rest of your life? Hell no! Will you put all the weight you lost back on when you go back to eating the way you did before? You can bet your last dollar that you will.

Gimmicks are designed to get you to spend your money on a product. That product will not heal your body, it won't solve your problem long-term. But the people selling it to you don't care. They have your money. As far as they're concerned, that transaction is over. If they're lucky, you'll make repeat purchases for a few months. But it's just a transaction. They are not concerned with your long-term well-being and overall health.

The reason these gimmicks fail is they're not sustainable. Nobody is going to just drink canned shakes for the rest of their lives, or exercise their daily calories away. A friend of mine told me her plan was to exercise off whatever calories she took in. The math sounded right to her. Calories in, calories out. Easy.

Guess what? In reality, 1,000 calories isn't a lot to eat; most people consume that much before lunch with their extra-large morning caramel macchiato and doughnut. But **IT'S A LOT OF WORK TO TRY AND EXERCISE OFF 1,000 CALORIES** every day, especially if you're overweight. That's a great way to blow out a knee!

If you're bound and determined to try this, at least be honest with yourself. Get a real heart rate monitor, one that straps on over your chest and counts your actual exertion. The little handles on the treadmill are not going to calculate your calories burned accurately. They are notorious for overestimating. And if it takes you an hour to burn 250 calories running on the treadmill...think about it. Are you really going to run FOUR HOURS a day? Seriously? Nobody has time for that, even if they could sustain it physically.

The All-Natural Myth

How many "all-natural" weight-loss products are out there? They seem to be endless. The truth is, marketing companies are smart. They know that you're more likely to try a product if it's all-natural. First of all, the labeling laws are pretty lax about what has to be in a product in order to use the term "all-natural." If they were to be 100% honest, the label would say "Um, maybe about 8% natural." The other thing is, just because something is all-natural doesn't necessarily mean it is good for you. Think about it, poison ivy is all-natural.

People have died from taking "all-natural" products, because they didn't know how they would interact with their bodies and any other medication or supplement they were taking at the time. This isn't to say that every all-natural product is going to kill you, but don't trust that something is good for you or safe just because of some marketing copy on the label. Educate yourself, and don't trust the marketing companies to have your best interests at heart.

Stimulants and Adrenal Fatigue

A lot of weight-loss products include stimulants. Caffeine, taurine, guarana— all these things stimulate the adrenal glands to produce adrenaline. When you're on an adrenaline high, you're not thinking about food. Too often, my clients come to me with adrenal problems. They've been taking a "health supplement," thinking it would help them lose weight.

When your adrenal glands have to work overtime in response to stimulants, whether that's too much coffee or actual stimulant drugs, they burn out. They stop working. And that produces amazing stress on the body which can lead to all sorts of other problems.

Ever heard of fen-phen? People lost weight on that stuff like nobody's business, because they never ate! We all know now how dangerous amphetamines are, but at the time people used them hoping to improve their lives. They lost weight all right—and a lot of them lost their teeth, too.

You don't need to pump chemicals into your body to lose weight. You don't.

There is one tried and true way to lose weight. Limit your intake to include only what nourishes your body. Make sure all those calories you consume are real food. Eat fat and protein. Eat veggies. Avoid sugar and processed foods, because those are what keep people from losing weight.

You don't need chemicals. You need real, nutritious food.

Shakes, Patches, and Other Bunk

So a lot of people complain that eating healthy is expensive. I think that's because their definition of food has been corrupted by decades of "diet aid" marketing campaigns. People duped by the weight-loss shake manufacturers are spending serious money on plans that are not going to work long-term.

Those suckers are **FULL OF SUGAR**. Just one shake can have 140 calories, and an entire day's worth of sugar and carbs. I can tell you one thing—that person is not going to be full after one shake. They will eat more during the day. And because they're eating all that sugar, they will crave more sugar. (Surprise! More shakes get sold.) It's not viable.

People sign up nonetheless, because they don't know that sugar is the real problem. And the manufacturers are only too happy to charge them $130 a month for one shake a day. No wonder people think "healthy" equals "expensive." What happens for those people when they're on the road? What do they eat when they don't have a shake in front of them? There's no sustainability.

Even the long-standing weight-loss clinics have the same problems. You can cheat the program and still technically be on plan. You can sit and eat candy all day, and as long as it's "approved" candy, the members think they're doing a good job. They are paying to be told that eating candy is going to help them lose weight. You have to kill the sugar addiction if you want to lose weight, and most clinics don't teach people how to do that.

Some of the products out there are just straight-up bogus. Weight-loss patches come to mind. Some folks sign up for these patches thinking they can just slap on a patch and they'll magically lose weight. Guess what? That doesn't work either.

The fact is, the reason none of these products work is that they offer quick fixes but don't correct what people are actually doing wrong. Your body gets the vitamins and minerals it needs from food. People become overweight because they are not eating the right food. Nobody needs any of these products. What people need is real, wholesome food. Why take an iron pill when you could just eat steak or broccoli?

Ask Yourself a Few Questions

Look, I'm not going to tell you what to do. If you enjoy spending tons of money on plans that deprive you of food, be my guest. But be honest with yourself! Are you really losing weight, and will you be able to keep it off forever?

The Code Red Lifestyle is based on evidence from over 700 individualized programs. We have a 98% success rate, and people keep the weight off for years after they leave the program. Do you want to stay on the hamster wheel? Or do you want to take control and change your body for good?

If you are embarking on a weight-loss program or thinking about using a product, ask yourself these questions:

- What's the sustainability? How long can you keep up whatever plan you're looking at?

- What are your goals? How much do you want to lose? Or do you just want to maintain?

- Where's the research to back up whatever product you're using?

- What are the ingredients? Will they interact with any medications you're taking?

- Is it a monthly membership you have to keep up with? Will you have to keep buying their product in order to stay on plan?

- Do you have to sell the product to other people to stay in, or to get discounted membership?

- Does it sound too good to be true? (Hint: It's probably just good marketing.)

I Get It

Trust me, I know how it feels to be desperate to make a change. I have worked with countless clients who would do anything to lose weight. If there were a patch or a magic pill, they would take it, no matter what the cost. And the diet industry knows that! It relies on that. It makes billions of dollars a year because it knows people will pay anything for hope.

But I am all about the truth. And the truth is, there is no magic pill. There is no quick fix.

The good news is that there is a way that will work. Code Red Rebels lose weight and keep it off. They heal their bodies and learn how to eat real food the right way. No shakes, no packets, no patches, powders, or pills.

The Code Red Lifestyle involves eating things like steak, bacon, eggs, avocados, and all the vegetables you could ever want. You get to eat real, delicious food. By learning how to eat the right nutrients the right way, Rebels lose weight and live healthier lives. Our skin glows, our joints don't hurt, and we love how we look and feel. All of this takes dedication, I'm not going to lie. You will have to adjust and get used to it. But that's the fun part!

It is not a gimmick, and you don't have to sell it to your friends (but you can totally share it with them). It just works.

Shelley Williams

Lost 78 Pounds in 3¹/₂ Months

I SHOULD START by saying that I was always athletic. I set records running track when I was in school—that kind of athletic. I've just always been a fit, active person. Then in 1986, a family member suffered a terrible accident. I took it particularly hard and was put on anti-depressants. Back then, those medications had some pretty serious side-effects. I put on 50 pounds in no time, and my struggle with weight began.

I quickly found that I couldn't do what I liked to do anymore. I couldn't run. I could barely get out to garden, and I *love* to garden. I couldn't go horseback riding, or at least I didn't because I felt that it wasn't fair to the horse. Worst of all, I couldn't run around and play with my grandkids. As the years went by, and my weight increased, I watched myself doing less and less.

It wasn't just my recreational life that suffered. My self-esteem went down as my weight went up. My knees hurt all the time. I had back problems. It all has a way of bringing you down, believe me.

My biggest health crisis came in 2002, when I suffered a case of Guillain-Barre syndrome. It's a nervous system auto-immune condition which, in extreme cases, can leave people paralyzed. It put me in the ICU for three months. I needed a feeding tube to eat and a trach tube to breathe.

I was in a coma-like state for several weeks and, while I eventually came out of it, I faced a lot of recovery time. You know how people often lose a ton of weight when they are in the hospital? Not me. I remember when they weighed me, after all that, I had only lost 7 pounds. I couldn't talk at the time, because I still had a trach tube in my neck, but I wanted to say, "Are you kidding me? I went through all that for 7 pounds!"

Fortunately, I made a full recovery, but I still couldn't lose weight. I tried every-thing—shots, shakes, fen-phen, Weight Watchers—every trick in the book. And even when I did lose 5 or 10 pounds, I always gained it back, with 5, 10, or 20 more. With my health issues, my business,

and the way I felt about myself, I was completely stressed out. The more I gained, the less active I became, and the more I ate to soothe my feelings.

WHEN IS IT GOING TO BE MY TURN?

I was at a family birthday party. We were all together to celebrate my mother-in-law's 80th birthday, and all the ladies in our family wore coordinating outfits. Well, the zipper on my dress busted open, and I had to run out to the store to try and find something that would look nice and match the family colors. When you're big like I was, clothes that fit aren't always easy to come by (let alone clothes that hide your fat). I was frustrated, embarrassed, and completely fed up.

I had watched my niece lose 40 pounds working with Cristy, and she said the plan was easy. A year later, my mother-in-law passed away, and I saw my niece at the funeral. She had lost even more weight, and I had put more on. That was my turning point. I looked at my niece and said to myself, "When is it going to be my turn?"

I was sick of not having the energy to do the things I liked to do. I had 4 beautiful grandchildren who I had no energy to play with. I couldn't help my husband around the ranch, because I was always too tired. I looked at my niece and said to myself, "If she can do it, I can too."

I decided it was finally *my* time.

NO WAITING AROUND

I thought I would start after New Year's Day, so I could go hit the buffet with family and celebrate, but Cristy wasn't having it. She had me start on December 27th. I had my doubts too, believe me. I had

tried *so* many other programs, and none of them had worked. Still, I saw with my own eyes what my neice was able to accomplish. I just told myself that I would do what Cristy said, and when I did that, the nutrition program was easy. I never felt like I was starving like on the other programs I had tried. I lost weight *fast*. It felt so good to see progress so quickly.

The rules are very simple, and Cristy is always there with you to help you stay on track. I didn't want to let her down. I didn't want to let my husband and family down again with *another* program I was trying. And most importantly, I didn't want to let *myself* down. I felt like I had been given my power back, and I wasn't about to fail.

The other things I tried, they focus on the diet or the plan. Cristy puts the focus on *you*. She makes you believe that you are strong and you don't need to cheat.

Early in my program, my grandson had a birthday party, and let me tell you, I *love* birthday cake. You know what I did? I took what I was going to eat into another room and stayed there until the tempting food was put away. It was hard, but I told myself, "I'm doing this for them." Being able to get on the floor and play with my grandson, or go ride bikes with him, is more important to me than eating cake with him. Once you make a decision like that, this program is easy.

I used to feel like I was starving on the diets I tried in the past, but this lifestyle doesn't do that to you. The biggest adjustment for me was cutting back on my snacking. I used to just eat whenever I walked by the cupboard or refrigerator because I felt like it. I don't do that anymore, and I don't miss it.

30 YEARS TO PUT IT ON— 3 MONTHS TO TAKE IT OFF!

As if I didn't have enough health issues to begin with, halfway through my weight-loss period, I ended up needing major surgery. It was supposed to require

anywhere from 6–8 weeks of recovery. The procedure itself was supposed to take at least 2 hours, but the surgeon ended up walking out after 45 minutes. My family thought something was wrong, but the doctor said, "Oh no, I'm done. It's much easier when the patient is slimmer." Thanks to the Code Red Lifestyle, I made it through that procedure quickly and without complications. With Cristy's support, I recovered quickly too.

I have lost a total of 78 pounds. It's still hard to believe. Despite health crises, deaths in the family, birthdays, holidays, and travel—I have lost 78 pounds!

My doctor couldn't believe it, my family couldn't believe it, and my friends were amazed. But Cristy never doubted that I could do it. I just met up with a friend of mine who I have known for 40 years, and she didn't even recognize me.

I have enjoyed without Cristy's constant support. Some people might have more willpower than me, but I can say from experience that working 1:1 with Cristy is worth every cent. When I think of what I used to spend on shots, pills, member-

I was 59 years old when I started this program, and I thought I was going to struggle the whole way. But it was easy, and now I have a whole new life to look forward to.

I was 59 years old when I started this program, and I thought I was going to struggle the whole way. But it was easy, and now I have a whole new life to look forward to. I can't thank Cristy and the rest of the Code Red community enough for helping me to take my life back. I would not have had the success that

ships, or doctor's visits, the cost of an individualized program is well worth it.

It took me 30 years to put all that weight on, but in just over 3 months on the Code Red Lifestyle, I took it off.

This works!

10 A Calorie is Not a Calorie

What's the Deal with Calories?

Calories.

Just the word is enough to make some people shiver. Calories have such a negative connotation, but they're highly misunderstood.

So what exactly is a calorie? There is a long, scientific definition, but basically, it's a unit of energy. It's not evil, it's not bad. It's just energy. You need calories to live. We can't function without a certain number of calories. So why are people so scared of them?

We all know that too many calories can make us fat, but that is only half the story. The typical Western diet is loaded with "empty calories." These are calories with no nutrients. They are manufactured foods that contain plenty of energy, but are also devoid of any wholesome substance. **EMPTY CALORIES ARE WHAT MAKE YOU FAT.**

You can actually starve yourself while eating loads of processed food, because you're eating calories without nourishing your cells. If your joints ache or your skin is bad, this could be why. You haven't been providing your body with the nutrition it needs to work at optimal performance.

So what happens? Your cells are crying out for nutrition, and **YOU'RE HUNGRY ALL THE TIME**. Sound familiar? You keep eating more and more processed junk, and your body never gets the nutrition it needs. So many Americans are incredibly sick because of this cycle. They're malnourished and fat at the same time. They're so hungry, even though they consume an enormous amount of food.

Our country wasn't always like this. Decades ago, we ate fewer calories but enjoyed higher nutrient levels. People from other countries don't have obesity problems like we do, mainly because their food is higher in nutrients than it is in calories. Before we became a fast-food nation, Americans were like that too. Heart disease, metabolic syndrome, and type II diabetes were not the problems they are now. People ate real food with real nutrients.

We have to get back to eating for nutrition.

Take an avocado for example. What is it? It's mostly fat. What is fat? Fat is energy, and calories are the units we measure the energy in. Fat actually has the highest energy yield of all the foods you eat. One gram of avocado has twice as much energy stored in it than a gram of grilled chicken breast. When you eat fat, you get more energy bang for your buck.

That's why Code Red Rebels eat fat!

An avocado is higher in calories than a scoop of fat-free ice cream, but it's not the avocado that will make you fat. There are carbs in an avocado (about 18g), but there's also a lot of fiber (about 15g). Fiber helps regulate the effects of the carbohydrate. In this example, you're only absorbing about 3g of carbohydrate. When you're figuring this out for yourself, you can simply subtract the grams of fiber from the grams of carbohydrate to find out how much sugar you're absorbing. This is called finding your "net carbs."

Even more importantly, that avocado has plenty of nutrients that your body needs to function at its best, like vitamin E, vitamin C, folate, and potassium. That fat-free ice cream? It has nothing. It's packed with sugar instead, which your body will store as energy (fat) for later. And you'll still feel hungry even after eating a large serving. An avocado, with all its fat, will nourish your body. The fat-free ice cream will leave your body starved. Avocados, bread, sugar-free ice cream—they all have calories. They're all forms of energy. However, the bread and the ice cream are empty calories. They give your body nothing except sugar to store in your body as fat.

I design carefully balanced nutrition plans for my clients for this very reason. Most people are used to consuming huge amounts of empty calories every day, including toxic levels of sugar and carbs. The Code Red Lifestyle flips that script. By eliminating the chemically engineered, manufactured food, you can heal your body by eating calories full of nutritious proteins and fats. You can heal your life with nutrient-rich calories.

There's a huge myth out there that all calories are equal, and that if you simply restrict your calories, you'll lose weight. Here's the deal. A calorie is not a calorie: 1,000 calories of cake is going to be processed completely differently than 1,000 calories of steak. And it will show up on your body completely differently. The cake is full of sugar and not much else. It goes to your liver, spikes your blood sugar, and your body stores those calories as fat. You feel high for a little while, then you crash and want another slice. The steak, on the other hand, has protein, fat, and other nutrients your body needs. There's a slow steady release of energy, with no spikes or crashes.

And one more thing—whether you burn a calorie running or sleeping, you've still burned a calorie. So the whole idea that you can just exercise away that piece of cake is a huge fallacy. I mean, in theory you can. But **YOU WOULD HAVE TO RUN FOR HOURS** to burn 1,000 calories. You'll blow out your knee (or your heart) before you ever get rid of that big slice of cake you ate last night.

Just don't eat the cake in the first place, m'kay? I know that's easier said than done. We'll talk more about how many calories you actually need in the next section. But by the end of this book, you'll know how to avoid those sugary empty calories without feeling deprived at all.

Kelsie Duman

This Nutrition Instructor and Busy Mom Turned Her Back on Conventional Wisdom and Finally Lost 37 Pounds

I WAS 180 pounds after having my second daughter. She had multiple health issues, and I was stuffing food in my face to deal with that stress. My doctor told me I was pre-diabetic, and the hospital sent me to a "healthy eating" course. There they taught me all about how I should be eating whole grains and having 5 meals a day—all the conventional wisdom we've been told for 40 years. And guess what? I lost 5 whole pounds after 12 weeks! My blood work was a little better, but I was still fat and miserable.

From that class, I was offered a job at the university teaching a nutrition class. So I just spread the same concepts and told people it was okay if they were overweight as long as they were eating healthy. I was teaching low-fat, whole-grain. And I just couldn't figure it out.

I reached out to Cristy and told her I thought I was overweight because I drank beer and liked fancy coffee. She told me, "Kelsie, you're overweight because you eat like crap!" It took a really long time to wrap my brain around the fact that everything I had been told was wrong, and I didn't need to eat that way. I don't need 5 meals a day. I'm totally fine with 1 or 2 a day.

I've always been a "happy person" but I was a fake happy. Inside I was just miserable and unhappy with myself. The biggest change is that I'm genuinely happy now. I don't have mood swings or grouchy spells. I'm a better mom this way.

And the water! I had a professional tell me that if I drank a gallon of water a day I was bleeding out all my salts and I was going to die. At first I was so scared to do that because that professional told me how bad it was. But now, I can't imagine not drinking my water. I love my water

I used to force myself to eat breakfast (yogurt with 40g of sugar and some granola). I would buy a caramel macchiato every single day. I also went for 5-mile walks with my kids, so I thought I could handle the sugar. These days, when I take a walk, it's "me time". I only do it if I want to, not because I need to burn fat.

It took a really long time for my husband to get on board because he kept telling me, "But you *know* how to lose weight. Just work out harder. That will help." But finally he could see the difference. I'm so

much happier. I'm a much better wife. And I don't freak out at him when he comes home late from work, because I've had the energy to keep up with the kids all day.

We used to eat at 8 p.m. every night, and that was just not good for my sleep.

I've always been a "happy person" but I was a fake happy. Inside I was just miserable and unhappy with myself. The biggest change is that I'm genuinely happy now. I don't have mood swings or grouchy spells. I'm a better mom this way.

I have a child with medical issues, and the hospital food was such a shock. You can walk down to the cafeteria and have pie and ice cream and all sorts of junk. I had to teach myself to always have my own food with me, just in case I couldn't find anything healthy to eat. Just a small package of nuts is all I need to tide me over. It would make me sick to drink the same amount of Dr. Pepper I drank a year and a half ago.

My kids are still very young. They have always been good eaters. Would they like to eat junk all the time? Sure. But that's not what they're used to. When my husband wants some chips, he keeps them out in the tractor. And now and then, the kids go out and have some. It's not a big deal. They just know we don't keep chips in the house. Ice cream is only for birthdays. If I bake cookies when their friends come over, they each get one or two and then they're gone. It's not tempting if it's not in the house. This is normal for us.

I didn't know anything about Cristy until a video popped up in my newsfeed. And I'll admit, at first I thought she was crazy. The things she was talking about I just knew were wrong. But then a little voice in my head said, "But look at all the people you know who follow her. And look at how much weight they've lost. They all feel great. Maybe there's something to this." So I sort of stalked her for 6 months before I started working with her.

It means so much to have someone who believes in you fighting for your success every day. And that's what Cristy and the other Rebels do. They are always there to support you and keep you on track, even when you feel like quitting. And let's face it, my husband gets a little tired of hearing me talk about every little victory on this journey. But the Code Red community celebrates with me when I say I'm wearing jeans I haven't worn since high school! They never get tired of hearing the good news. And that's so encouraging.

The best part is, it's easy. I'm eating the foods I love and nothing I don't. I'm not exercising so hard that I can't walk up the stairs in my house. I'm not grouchy with my kids. It's the best thing I've done for myself, and I'm so grateful to have found this lifestyle.

THE
CODE RED
PROGRAM

The Code Red Program:

How to Lose the Weight Without Being Hungry

WHEN I MEET WITH A PRIVATE CLIENT, I do a thorough workup on their individual health. I write up a personalized nutrition program. And I monitor them daily to make sure they follow it to the letter (more on that in a bit).

But I don't know your personal background. I don't know what you're sensitive to. I don't know if dairy makes your tummy hurt, or if you're a vegetarian.

So I'm going to give you the basics of my program here. And then I'll show you how to modify the recommendations to suit your needs, your taste, and your life. Most importantly, I'll show you exactly what to do to keep that weight off for good.

Most weight-loss books give you specific instructions—meals to eat, recipes you're "allowed" to use, phases, and math formulas. If you haven't figured it out yet, this book is different. This plan is sustainable for your entire life, not just while you're losing weight. All you have to do to lose all the weight you want—and keep it off for good—is follow 7 simple rules.

Now, when I say follow the rules, I mean **FOLLOW THE DAMN RULES!**

You are strong.

You are a Rebel.

You keep to the code and don't stray. There's never an excuse to go off the plan. We don't believe in cheat days. We don't take weekends off. We don't stray just because it's someone's birthday.

Look, it's always someone's birthday, or Christmas, or an anniversary, or something! You're going to get stressed. Loved ones will get sick and even die. Jobs will suck. Life isn't going to stop just because you're trying to lose weight. The world isn't going to stop turning. So that means you have to figure out how to stick to the rules in spite of whatever is going on in your life. The second you let yourself slide on one meal, it's a quick ride to a full-on binge. Or worse, you just give up altogether.

No. We don't do that. One cheat will set you back a week of progress. If you don't think you can do this without cheating, think again! **YOU CAN DO THIS.** You will need support, and that's why we have a strong community of Rebels. Every one of them has looked temptation and birthday cake in the eye and won. Every one of them has had a tough day now and then, days when they needed to vent and hear someone tell them to stay strong.

You want cheat days and gimmicks and sloooow weight loss?
Find another program.

You want this time to be the **LAST TIME** you ever have to do this?
Follow the Code Red Lifestyle.

I know there's a good chance you've tried other ways to lose weight and failed. There's a good chance that deep down you are really afraid you'll fail again. That's normal. Please listen to me, though. You're not just learning a new set of eating rules. You're transforming both your body and your mind. You're choosing a path and sticking with it. When you make that kind of commitment, with the support of like-minded people, and you have a solid plan, you cannot fail!

What Should Your Goal Weight Be?

If you're like most people I talk to, you've been thinking about your so-called ideal weight since like 5th grade. Your doctor is telling you one thing. Your insurance company might be telling you something different. There are government charts and scientific theories about what an ideal weight is for someone of your height. The magazines and TV advertising show you photo-shopped models who are impossibly thin. Who knows how much those chicks actually weigh or what their thighs actually look like? There's so much conflicting information out there, how are you supposed to know what the heck your goal should really be?

One thing I've noticed is when I ask my clients what weight they think they should be shooting for, it's almost always 20 or 30 pounds higher than what I know they can achieve. They will pick a weight they know they can reach because they did it 10 years ago when they did Weight Watchers and went to Jazzercize twice a day. They'll pick something they think is realistic for them. If someone is 5' 6" and they should be around 145, they'll say "Okay, 175 sounds good to me!" I have to tell them no, they can do better than that.

In the beginning, it's hard to believe when I tell them they can get down to where they were in high school. Some people have been overweight for so long, they don't even remember being a healthy weight. I get that. It's okay. Just realize that you can set "for now" goals. If you're 250, set a "for now" goal of 225 or 199. Then you can set another goal and another—as many as you need to get down to a number you can naturally maintain without a lot of struggle.

You can't hit a goal if you don't know what it is. So before we go into the rules, I want to help you get really clear on what number you want to hit during the weight-loss phase of this lifestyle. I've discovered something over the course of supervising over 700 weight-loss programs: everyone is different! There's no magic formula for what your weight should be. And you know what else? Your body intuitively knows where it wants to be. It knows your number, and it might just shock the hell out of you when you figure out what it is.

Rather than looking outside yourself for your goal weight, try looking inward. Close your eyes and think back to a time when you were happy and you felt alive, strong, and healthy. When was the last time you felt truly sexy? It might be when you got married. Or maybe you were happy with your weight when you graduated high school. Now, about how much did you weigh then?

It's critical that you don't judge yourself on whatever number you come up with! If you currently weigh over 200 pounds, and you know you weighed 125 in high school, your gut reaction might be "Who the heck do you think you are? You'll never get back to that weight. That's in the past. You can't possibly get down to your high school weight. Stop aiming so high!"

But here's the thing—it could be that 125 is totally realistic for you. If that number feels good and right, then that should be your goal. Don't listen to that voice in your head telling you it's impossible.

You must feel good about the number you choose, even if it seems like you'll never get there. If you **KNOW IN YOUR HEART** that you felt amazing at 125—go for it! As you lose weight over time, your body is going to settle in right at the number where it wants to be. There will be a place where you no longer have to struggle. A natural weight you can easily maintain.

Remember when I said everyone is different? Maybe 125 is the perfect place for you. Or 115. Or 165. Or 195. I don't know what your ideal weight is...and neither do you, right now. But you need to have a goal to shoot for. So it might as well be a goal that you have happy associations with.

As I mentioned, most people I work with set their goal weights higher than I think they should. They really want to be 140, but they can't remember a time when they weighed that little. So they shoot for 165. And that's totally fine! If they can recall feeling happy, healthy, and sexy at 165, that's a perfect goal. What often happens is they reach that goal and start living the Code Red Lifestyle in maintenance mode, but they keep losing weight! They don't understand it. They go lower and lower without even trying. It's because they've healed their bodies with real, nutritious food. They're sleeping enough

and drinking enough water. And their bodies know where they want to settle. Maybe it's 150. Maybe it's 140, a number they couldn't even say out loud when they started.

You might also choose an initial goal that's too low. You'll know if that's the case because it will be really hard to stay at that weight. Your body will naturally want to settle a little higher. And that's fine, too. The number on the scale is just a tool. It does not define who you are or what you're worth. You need the numbers to measure your progress. The direction the scale is moving is what matters. Are you going up or down compared to yesterday? After a while, the actual numbers don't really matter at all.

Your body is wise. It knows where you should be. So for now, set a goal that makes you happy. Just realize that might not be where you end up.

What is "Real Food" Anyway?

Processed food is anything you eat that has gone through a mechanical process before it gets to you, or comes from a bag, a can, or a box. It's food that has to be preserved somehow to be shelf-stable for long periods of time. Often it contains artificial chemicals and sugar to help improve flavor and texture, and preserve it for a longer shelf life.

Real food, on the other hand, appears in your grocery store pretty much like nature made it. Fruits and vegetables look more or less the same when you buy them as they did when they were picked. A steak has been through the butchering process, but it's still considered real food if the only ingredient on the label is beef. Breaded chicken nuggets, on the other hand, are highly processed, chemical-filled concoctions that may or may not have any actual chicken in them.

Food manufacturers want to sell you "food products," and they want to *keep* selling you "food products." They hire scientists to make them look, taste, and smell like real food. They hire scientists to make them addictive, too. The food-like products they engineer have the addiction built in to keep you buying. They'll market low-fat ice cream as healthy, but they'll add twice as much sugar as regular ice cream just to keep you eating it.

Have you heard of MSG? It's short for monosodium glutamate, and it is in 80% of the processed "foods" available to the average shopper. Hop online and google "MSG-induced obesity." To study obesity in mice, scientists feed them MSG to make them obese. Why are Americans eating what scientists give to mice with the purpose of making them obese? Your body doesn't need that. It doesn't need energy drinks, soda, high sodium, processed "food" juice, or alcohol. What your body needs is real food!

Here again, you've got to get used to reading labels and looking for the added sugar and chemicals. Frozen broccoli is technically a processed food. It comes in a bag. It's been through the flash-freezing process. But the only ingredient on the label is broccoli. So it's considered a real food. It was broccoli in the field, and it's still broccoli, just frozen.

And what's cool about frozen veggies is they often have higher levels of vitamins and minerals than the fresh versions in the produce section. That's because as soon as plants are harvested, they begin to lose their nutrients. So if it takes a week to get that broccoli from the farm to your table, there may not be much vitamin content left. But when it's frozen right after it's picked, the freezing process preserves the vitamins and minerals until you eat it.

When you give your body nutritious, real food, it's not going to tolerate the processed, sugary junk food as much anymore. My stomach hurts after those rare occasions when I eat processed food. You will eventually find that you just don't want that stuff anymore. Instead of telling yourself you can't have that food, you'll be telling yourself you don't want it. And that's a beautiful thing.

That is the difference between good nutrition and a diet. Telling yourself "I can't have that" leads to a diet mentality. Diets have failure built into them; that's why there are so many of them. They're products, not lifestyles. On the other hand, **NUTRITION IS JUST GIVING YOUR BODY WHAT IT'S SUPPOSED TO HAVE**. Once you do that, you can feed yourself fast food if you want, but your body won't like it. Instead of "I can't have" you will be saying, "I can. But I don't want it."

You will find that the Code Red Lifestyle is completely doable. It's not rocket science. All you're doing is reading labels and eating real food. By staying away from the processed garbage that our society is addicted to, you are healing your body. We live in a society that is overfed but undernourished.

THE VOICES IN YOUR HEAD

The voices are real! They are the parts of us that keep us safe and alive. They each have a job to do. Unfortunately, the ones that keep us stuck are usually the loudest.

What's wrong with me? Why can't I do this? I'm so weak!

Does any of that sound familiar?

Here's how to solve the "voices" problem: Don't try to defeat them, get them all talking to each other. Get them on the same page, working toward the same goal!

Try This Exercise

Imagine the voices as real people and give them each a voice. Hold a "board meeting" and let them say whatever they want to say. Literally sit in a chair, become one of the voices, and talk. Then move to another chair, be the next voice, and let that one have their say. Move back and forth between chairs as long as you need to. Have a real conversation with yourself.

And remember, you are the one in charge. The negative voice may be loud, but **YOU ARE THE ONE IN CONTROL**. The cheerleader's voice may be quiet, but you can choose to ask her to repeat herself over and over again, louder and louder.

If it feels weird to have a conversation out loud, you can write it out instead. Use different colors for the different voices. The point is to realize that you are having this conversation unconsciously all the time. These voices are ruling your life...but it doesn't have to be that way! **YOU GET TO DECIDE WHEN** enough is enough. But you can't just lock the voices in a closet or stuff them down deep inside you—they know when you're weak, and they'll always come back. So instead, let them talk, thank them for their viewpoints, and then you decide which voice to listen to.

Willpower isn't enough. You have to make a decision. **THIS IS THE LAST TIME YOU'RE GOING AROUND THIS MOUNTAIN!**

All those boxes and bags on the shelves? They're not food. Those food-like products are the result of food companies taking sales to the laboratory.

There are no secrets. Marketers and the diet industry want us to think there's a "Hollywood secret" or a "hunter/gatherer secret." You may even think this book is about a "Code Red secret."

Listen to me—there are no secrets!

Even though we are all unique individuals, every single person on this planet is designed to eat and metabolize food the same basic way. Sometimes things go wrong and we're born with genetic problems, or we mess up our systems somehow. If you're lactose intolerant or celiac or don't have a gallbladder, you might need to change your intake a little bit.

But in general, everyone from Oprah Winfrey to Bob Jones has to follow the same set of rules. There is no secret set of rules for celebrities. We all have the same basic biology. And we can fix a lot of physical problems and diseases by returning to simple nutrition and real food, and using up all that energy (fat) we've stored for later.

Angie & Mike Stegner

Grief, Heartbreak, and Triumph

I'VE BATTLED with food practically my whole life. It's just always been a way to comfort myself anytime I was feeling down or just bored. Then I had children, and that put more weight on. Then we found out my daughter, Morgan, was chronically ill with a heart defect, and all my focus went to helping her. She was always on special diets, and to encourage her to eat, we ate the same things. In this case, that meant a no-fat diet. I was eating all kinds of garbage, just because it was low-fat.

In the end, Morgan lost her battle. I used food to numb my intense grief, and all the anger and emotions showed up as fat on my body. I started eating everything I couldn't eat on Morgan's diet—all the ice cream and fried foods I could get my

Every day she would say,

"I want to live. I want to live."

I remember promising her,

"I will live for you."

Except I wasn't. I wasn't living for her.

I was killing myself with food.

hands on. Every hard milestone—her birthday, the holidays, and the anniversary of her death—I would eat and drink just to get through it.

I have always been transparent with the loss of my child and now my weight loss. I felt so alone when it happened because I knew no one personally who had lost a child, especially one so young. I felt so alone and vowed to help anyone not be as isolated and alone as I was. She was 8 years old when she died, and she wanted to live so badly.

I realized that I was killing myself because my daughter had died. That hit me like a ton of bricks. She wouldn't have wanted that. And I realized I was being selfish. I wanted to give her the life she couldn't have. And our other children had been

denied a mom for so long. They deserved to have a happy, healthy mom.

I stepped on the scale one day and saw that I was 199. I'm 5'2", and at that weight I was almost as wide as I was tall. Then I saw a photo of myself in Las Vegas, and

I was *mortified* that I looked so large. Shortly after that, someone at a family function said, "Wow, you've gained some weight." All those things piled on and helped me make a decision to change.

TAKING MY LIFE BACK

I joined the 10-Pound Takedown challenge, but waited until the last minute to sign up because I didn't want to fail. I've known Cristy since high school, and I'd been following her progress and how well people do on her program. But I had tried to lose weight so many times with pills and shakes and all the gimmicks. I would lose 5 pounds and then stop. I just didn't want to fail again.

When I signed up, I had just broken my leg and was unable to exercise. So Cristy's promise of weight loss with no exercise was almost like a challenge to me. I couldn't have exercised if I wanted to, so it was a good test. I figured if I failed, at least I would be proving her wrong.

I'm married to a police officer. If you know anything about that job, you know there's no shortage of stress! He is my second husband and not Morgan's dad. He had to learn to love me broken and never once pressured me to lose weight. What's more, he never once pretended

to know how deep my grief ran. So when I told him that I had made a promise to Morgan to live for her and be the kind of happy she had been, it clicked with him.

Mike was also struggling with his weight. I didn't really think he'd join me. But I decided I was going to try the Code Red Lifestyle for myself. I would cook one meal, and if the rest of the family didn't want to eat it, they could find something else to eat.

Mike hates vegetables, but after a short time he started really liking the meals I prepared. And once he discovered he was losing weight, he was all in! We even went so far as to dump every bottle of alcohol in the house down the drain.

Our girls are still pretty young, and they're not following the lifestyle 100%. But that's okay. I'm just happy they're seeing that there's a different way to eat, and that their mom and dad are getting healthy.

I've noticed some amazing things happening with my family. I have a wacky schedule and have to get up at 3 a.m. to go to work. Since I've quit the sugar and the coffee drinks, I get up easier and I have steady energy all day long. I don't have the energy highs and lows that I used to. I can think more clearly, and I don't get angry as quickly. My mood is stable.

SOME ADVICE FOR BABY REBELS

If you're thinking about diving into this way of life, I say go for it! Keep an open mind. I had lots of questions and doubts at the beginning, too. I wanted to make it more complicated than it really is because that would make it easy for me to quit. Trust the process. It works.

Don't compare yourself to others. It's so frustrating to me that Mike loses a pound a day, even when he doesn't get all his sleep or water. And I'll follow the rules perfectly, and might be up a half pound the next day. You can't control how fast other people lose, so just keep focused on *your* progress and your success.

Be flexible. Sometimes you have to adjust according to how your body feels. I know there are Code Red Approved foods that my body just can't tolerate. And that's okay. I just don't eat them. I've taken my life back, and I'm in control.

Rely on the Code Red community. Whenever I'm frustrated or have a question or want to give up, all I have to do is log on and say something. People will immediately jump on and encourage me to keep going. And being able to

support others is helpful, too. We're all in this together.

My life experience has made me who I am. And even knowing how it played out, I would do it all again. Being Morgan's mom was a great joy and privilege of my life. My faith and strength from loving her and losing her has taught me that I am incredibly blessed.

I honestly believed that I could hide behind my pain and use it to justify what I had become. Cristy taught me that was unnecessary, that I was worth more, and that pain and grief didn't define me!

Today our life is good. Our love is so authentic and genuine. I love our story. Mike is my hero in so many ways, and Cristy is my (s)hero!

12 Here Are the Rules

1. Sleep at least 7–8 hours every night.

2. Drink at least one gallon of water per day.

3. Weigh yourself every morning.

4. Don't eat past 6:30 p.m.

5. Weigh, measure, and log everything that goes into your mouth.

6. Keep the junk out of your house.

7. Follow the Foods to Eat / Foods to Avoid list.

Here Are the Details

I don't know about you, but I hate rules when I don't know why I have to follow them. Rebels will rebel. It's in our nature. So I want to help you understand why these are the rules and why **YOU MUST NOT BREAK THEM**. If you're serious about taking your life back, these are non-negotiable during weight-loss mode. We'll talk about how to keep yourself on track in a little bit. But first, you've got to understand the why.

RULE #1: **Sleep at least 7–8 hours every night.**

When you don't get enough sleep, your body senses that as stress. And it can't tell the difference between stress because you're being chased by a saber-toothed tiger and stress from a long work commute. Stress is stress. And the first thing your body does to protect itself is hang onto fat. Fat means survival to your body.

My dad is a licensed counselor, and we go round and round on this topic all the time. His clients really struggle with sleep, and so do mine. But he believes that some people can function just fine on 5 or 6 hours a night. My experience has been that if people get fewer than 7 hours, their weight loss stalls out.

I think the key word here is "function." Can you function on less sleep? Sure you can. You've learned coping mechanisms and trained yourself to manage that way—maybe even for years. Perhaps you've even convinced yourself that you're just one of those people who don't need very much sleep.

But I know that when I get fewer than 7 hours a night, I get cranky easier. My skin starts to get blotchy and cellulite starts to show up. I notice my stress levels going up and my weight might go up too. What's worse, I start to crave sugar.

Here's a word of warning for all you night owls and last-minute deadline workers: lack of sleep will increase sugar cravings. Recently, I have not gotten enough sleep. I've been staying up late taking care of clients who are on Pacific Time, working on my business, and really running low on sleep. If I sleep less than 6 hours, I don't do too well. When you add in my gym schedule and everything else I have to do, I just hit a wall.

What happens when you don't get enough sleep? It goes something like this:

Your body says, "Hey, listen. You're hitting a wall. It's not looking good. You need to get some sleep."

And you say, "Hey. I've got crap to do. We've got to keep going."

Your body isn't stupid. It knows exactly what's going to happen. But you are pretty stubborn, and you keep pushing. So your body says, "Okay. If that's the way you really want it, that's fine. If you're not going to sleep, then we've got to get some quick fuel in here to keep you going. You need a pick-me-up."

And that's when the sugar cravings kick in. It's just chemistry. It's how we're made. We make demands on our bodies, and we have to have fuel to support those demands. When we burn the candle on both ends, that fuel often comes in the form of sugar. A quick hit on a caramel macchiato. Oh, and you want to throw in a cookie with that? Sure, why not? You're working hard, you deserve it!

You will get that sugar high. The energy will be there for a little while. Then you're going to crash, and your energy will be lower than ever. If you keep ignoring your body, you'll need more and more sugar to keep going. Your weight will creep up. Your body will start to cramp and hurt. All because your body is crying out, "Hey! Take care of me! You're treating me like crap."

I can go years without a sugar craving. But sure enough, when I push myself too far, they'll come back. And it's all too easy to fall into the downward spiral of sugar highs and lows. It's not worth it.

Starting right now, I want you to pay attention to your body. What does it really need? When it says, "Hey! Caramel macchiato! You need a dough-nut. You just need a pick-me-up," that's your cue to pay attention. Because that's a craving talking. And cravings are signs that your body really needs something else. Maybe it needs sleep. Maybe it needs some water. Maybe it needs to spend an evening laughing with friends. What it *doesn't* need is another doughnut.

It's okay to talk back to your body. You do it all the time when you ignore its warning signs. So next time those cravings show up and you just know you're pushing yourself too hard, try saying this:

> Hey there, body. Thanks for clueing me in. You're right. I am
> pushing you really hard. I have one errand left to do, and then
> I'll go home and take a nap. Okay? Help me get through this
> next hour, and I will reward you with that sleep you need.

Maybe, just maybe—if you speak nicely to your body and treat it with kindness—it won't even bother sending those cravings. Because you don't need that doughnut. Not even just one.

I know there are a lot of extra demands on you; everybody has them. But trust me. Don't run low on sleep. You're not doing yourself any favors. You're setting yourself up to fight a battle with your body. And you already know the craving battle is practically impossible to win.

So follow the rules and get at least 7 hours a night, even if that means you have to rearrange your life a little bit. Your body will thank you!

RULE #2: Drink a gallon of water every day.

What if I told you the one secret to losing weight and keeping it off? What if I told you it wasn't exercise? It's not shakes and pills. It isn't a diet. What if

I told you it was free? It is available to you right now, and you can start seeing results and feeling better immediately.

What if I told you that? Would you believe me?

I've been in this industry since 1994. I competed in three body-building competitions. While studying exercise physiology at the University of Memphis, I took up professional boxing as a way to pay for books and tuition. And I was named one of the top three most dangerous females on the planet. I've written hundreds of nutrition programs for people all over North America. So yeah. I know what I'm talking about when it comes to nutrition and losing weight. And I want you to hear the truth.

You ready for my non-secret?

WATER.

Let me say that again.

Water.

Drink at least a gallon of water every day.

It sounds simple, doesn't it? It sounds too good to be true, I know. It's not. There are so many positive correlations between water consumption and good health. Not only does it help your hair and nails grow, but it also helps you sleep. It helps regulate hormones. It gives you energy. It's going to keep you full and satiated for long periods of time.

Water consumption is absolutely key to weight loss and keeping your weight down. Try it. You won't want to have caramel macchiatos. You won't want the candy, the cake, or the other unhealthy treats you normally crave.

Why haven't you heard how much just plain old water can help with your weight loss? Because there's no money in it. Water is free. (Thank goodness!)

Here's the deal—when you're thirsty, your body sends signals that it's hungry. So, very often you eat instead of drinking. But 9 times of out 10, you're not hungry. You are just dehydrated.

Here are some of the main benefits of drinking a gallon of water a day:

YOU'LL FEEL FULL. And there won't be room in your tummy for the junk.

YOUR BODY WILL FLUSH OUT TOXINS. Your kidneys eliminate toxins and waste products from the blood and urine, and process water-soluble toxins from the liver. If you don't drink enough water, your kidneys won't have enough fluid to function properly.

YOU'LL HAVE AMAZING ENERGY. The number one reason for daytime fatigue is dehydration. So staying hydrated may help you have more energy. And since your brain is mostly water, drinking plenty of it helps you concentrate and be more alert.

YOU'LL SLEEP BETTER. Staying hydrated allows your brain to work at its best, even when "working" means "resting." A well-hydrated brain lets you enjoy a good night's sleep and wake feeling rejuvenated and ready for the day ahead.

YOUR SKIN WILL CLEAR UP. Drinking water keeps your skin moisturized, fresh, soft, glowing, and smooth. (Psst! Good hydration also helps get rid of wrinkles.)

YOUR HAIR WILL BE HEALTHIER. If your hair follicles lack water, your hair will become dry and brittle. This gradually slows down and even stops the growth of your hair.

Now, a gallon of water is a lot to drink if you're not used to it, but it's completely safe. Can you drink too much water? Yes. It's called hyponatremia. Your electrolyte balance gets out of whack.

The rule of thumb is that you need half your body weight in ounces of water just to maintain minimal body function like tear ducts, sweat glands, urination, saliva, etc. To aid in weight loss, you want to add to that because you're cutting out all the energy drinks, sweet tea, and even water-filled fruits that you normally consume. So you need to add the water to thrive.

A gallon of water is 128 ounces, which is a pretty safe amount for most people. If you're exerting yourself on a really hot day, your body may ask you to drink more water. Listen to your body.

Some people don't like the taste of water. I hear that from my clients all the time. There are a few good ways to get all those ounces down easier. One simple way is to use a straw. Straws make you drink faster. (Why do you think restaurants give you straws? So you'll finish the first drink quickly and order another one.) You can also add sugar-free drops to improve the flavor. Here's what you can use without adding sugar to your water: lemon slices or lemon juice, lime slices or lime juice, or orange slices. Do not use orange juice— that's just adding sugar.

Don't be tempted to turn your water into Kool-Aid. Even the sugar-free addi-tives are so full of chemicals that you're not doing your body any favors. I like to use Mio water flavoring drops. They come in lots of flavors, you can get them at the grocery store, and they taste really good. You only need a tiny bit to make your water taste better. But be aware that some people are sensitive to the artificial sweeteners in these drops. If you find yourself craving more sugar or your weight loss stalls, stop using the drops and see if that fixes the problem. For a more natural approach, throw an herbal tea bag in your water.

Water. It's simple. It's free. It's available. It starts working immediately. Drink a gallon of water today and each day after that. I promise you will thank me for it.

RULE #3: Weigh yourself every morning.

People have a love/hate relationship with the scale. No matter what number shows up, they either feel happy or they beat themselves up. Conventional wisdom says you should only weigh yourself once a week or even once a month. Code Red Rebels weigh themselves every single day. Even when they're traveling or on vacation. (We pack travel scales, in case you were wondering.)

Daily weigh-ins are part of the Code Red Lifestyle because the scale is your first line of defense. It's your first clue that you're either on track or you may need to tweak something you're doing. If you only weigh yourself once a week, and your weight goes up, how are you supposed to figure out what went wrong? If you binged on a bag full of Oreos earlier in the week, it's pretty obvious what happened. But what if you did everything right? It's really hard to figure out what's going on if you have to analyze 7 days' worth of data. But if your weight goes up after just one day, it's pretty easy to see what's happening. Maybe you didn't get enough sleep, or you fell behind on your water. Maybe you ate some soy sauce with your veggie stir-fry and the sodium sent your weight up. Or maybe you're just really stressed out at work.

I had one client whose weight suddenly went up for a few days in a row. She was logging everything, and getting all her sleep. It didn't make sense that she was gaining. We looked at her log carefully and noticed that she had just started using the Mio water flavorings. Now, most people can use that stuff just fine. But for her, the sweet taste made her want it all the time. So instead of a tiny bit in her water now and then, she was using a lot of it in every bottle of water she drank. I had her cut that stuff out, just as an experiment, and sure enough her weight came right back down.

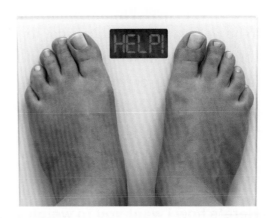

If she had waited to weigh in for a week or two, who knows if we would have figured it out so quickly? She might have continued to gain, lost confidence, and quit the program altogether. Instead, we were able to troubleshoot the problem in just a day or two. She recognized exactly why she was gaining. Something weird was happening and we just had to figure it out. There was no stress, and no blaming herself for being "bad" or "screwing up." We just worked the problem. Pretty refreshing compared to most diets, don't you think?

Remember when I said that the only thing that matters is the *direction* the scale is moving? That is the 100% truth. The actual number doesn't mean anything. Let's say you made a mistake and had a margarita the night before and now you're up a pound. If you see that first thing in the morning, guess what? You're going to buckle down and make sure you're following the rules today. You're going to course correct immediately. If you wait for a week, who knows how much damage you'll do before you get back in control. Daily weighing means daily accountability.

Daily weighing also means that you will eventually make peace with your scale. Remember, this is a lifestyle, not a diet. Which means you're going to be weighing yourself every day for the rest of your life, ideally. Even when you're at goal weight, the scale is still your first line of defense. So rather than hating the scale, or getting mad at it, after a while it's just going to be a thing you do first thing in the morning. No big deal. The numbers will eventually cease to grab hold of you and affect your whole day. It might take a while, but at some point, your scale will become a companion—not a source of shame or guilt, and not something to obsess over.

Here's how I want you to weigh yourself.

First, get yourself a good digital scale, one that weighs down to the ounce. If your bathroom scale is 10 years old, do yourself a favor and get a new one. You deserve it. This little guy is going to be with you for an amazing journey. Every morning when you wake up, go potty to get rid of the water you drank yesterday. Then strip down naked and weigh in. Do this *before* you eat or drink anything!

And when I say naked, I mean it. My mom even takes her Fitbit off because she swears that thing weighs a pound. Then as soon as you weigh in, log your weight. My clients have to log it in the Lose It app so I can check them every morning. But you can keep a little notebook by your bed, or print out our weight-tracking sheet from the resources page at the back of this book. It's up to you. The important thing is to do it every single day.

What happens if you're up from the day before? We'll talk about that in a little bit. There are very specific reasons for a weight gain. And once you know how to troubleshoot what's happening, you'll know exactly what to do to fix the problem without blame, shame, or guilt. For now, though, let's keep going through the rules.

RULE #4: Don't eat past 6:30 p.m.

This one rule is probably the one that gets the most pushback from my clients. Why 6:30? Is it like Cinderella? Will you magically turn back into a pumpkin if you eat past 6:30?

I struggle to find an answer to this one because I get that it doesn't make sense. The technical answer is that you want to go to bed a little bit hungry. You want your body to be done with the major digestive functions by the time you go to sleep, so it can focus on all the other processes it has to do at night like deep healing and hormone regulation.

Some people say, "Can't I just make sure I eat 3 hours before I go to bed?" And you would think that's a reasonable solution. But my years and years of experience say no. If it were up to me, I'd have everyone finish eating even earlier, like 5 p.m. I usually finish my last meal at 4:00. (But then, I'm usually in bed by 8:00.)

There's just something about 6:30. It's the latest time I can push and have people still lose weight the next day. Every time I have a client come to me wondering why they didn't lose the night before, if they tell me they ate at 7:00

or 8:00, that's the answer. Every time. Even if they went to bed later. I don't know why it is. It just is.

If you work the night shift, or you typically stay up past midnight, first make sure you're getting enough sleep. Then adjust that 6:30 number to be *at least* three hours before your normal bedtime. I would prefer you eat 4 or even 5 hours before.

Remember, the goal is steady weight loss. You can even see a drop on the scale every single day. Just follow the rules, and your weight will go down.

RULE #5: Weigh, measure, and log everything that goes into your mouth.

Okay, this one isn't going to be a rule forever. It's just for weight-loss mode. But it is a **NON-NEGOTIABLE RULE**! Measure and log everything that goes into your mouth. Every. Thing. That means down to the last Tic Tac and piece of gum. (Did you know sugar-free gum actually has 2g of carbs? I didn't until recently.)

You'll need to buy a digital food scale, which are like $10 on Amazon. You're going to need a couple of sets of measuring spoons, one for the house and one for the car. Yes, you're going to measure everything you eat on the road (even at restaurants). You're also going to need some measuring cups.

One reason I love the Lose It app is because items are easy to log. They have a huge database full of all kinds of foods and recipes. And it even has a handy barcode scanner. So if you don't feel like typing in the nutrition label on your favorite salad dressing, you can just scan the barcode and it will pop right up.

You're logging so you can keep track of your calories and your macronutrient ratios. Just like weighing every day, your food log helps you troubleshoot before things get out of hand. Everyone has different circumstances. I create completely custom programs for my clients based on their height, weight, activity levels, stress levels, and more. But I want you to have a baseline to shoot for, so here's about where you want to be to lose weight without being hungry.

60% OF YOUR DAILY CALORIES FROM FAT

30% OF YOUR DAILY CALORIES FROM PROTEIN

10% OF YOUR DAILY CALORIES FROM CARBOHYDRATES

NO MORE THAN 25G OF TOTAL SUGAR

That's it. That's all you need to think about. If you're logging in an app, the ratios should be calculated for you.

People often ask me how many calories they should consume every day. I really can't tell you that in a book like this. Because every client I serve is different. What I *can* tell you is to make a close connection with your body. Listen to it carefully. It will tell you when it's full and when it's hungry. Your brain will try to trick you with "emotional hunger," which is when you aren't really hungry, but you just *want* that bag of chips. Don't fall for this one!

If you stick to your macros, you should level out at the right number of calories for you to lose weight without being hungry or experiencing cravings. However, if you are following the rules exactly, and your weight still isn't going down, try an experiment and lower your calories a bit. Like, maybe just lower them by 250 or 500. And see what happens to your weight. If you're afraid that you'll be hungry, remember that the fat is going to keep you full. Some of my clients discover they can eat up to 80% of their calories from fat, which satiates their hunger and allows them to keep their calories low. Sometimes you just have to experiment and see what works.

Here's another huge secret to weight loss...

Seriously, this will blow your mind and change your life forever...

Are you ready?

Log everything you plan to eat that day first thing in the morning!

Let that sink in for a moment.

What most people do, if they're logging and tracking at all, is they eat a meal and then write down what they ate. Their first mistake is they're not weighing exactly—they're just guessing—and we always underestimate how much things really weigh. If you're following the rules and think you're doing everything right, but still are not losing weight, sloppy measuring is often the culprit.

Here's the deal—if you log your meals before you eat, you have a chance to fix a mistake or a cheat before you do any damage. Let's say you have a date tonight. You're in weight-loss mode, so you pick a restaurant where you're sure there's something on the menu that you're allowed to eat. When you get there, you decide to go for the broiled salmon with asparagus. And you even remember to log it in before you go to bed. You feel great! You navigated a restaurant, had a great time, and stuck to your diet.

The next day, you're up 3 pounds! What the heck? You did everything right, didn't you?

Well, not exactly.

Mistake number one was not weighing the food. How much did you *actually* eat? Sure, salmon and asparagus are healthy choices. But you have no idea how many calories you actually consumed. If you don't want to pull out your travel food scale (they fit in your pocket, seriously)—then you can at least ask the server how many ounces the fish and veg are. They might need to go ask the kitchen, but they should be able to tell you.

Mistake number two was not accounting for the oil, butter, or other sauces the food was cooked with. Did you eat broiled salmon or fried? Were those asparagus spears slathered in butter before they went into the oven? There's nothing wrong with food cooked in fats. (In fact, it's preferable, as long as they are healthy fats.) But you need to log that stuff too. The calories add up. What you might have logged as a 500-calorie dinner could easily have been 2,500 calories in reality. Once again, the math is keeping you fat.

Mistake number three was not logging everything first thing in the morning. This date was planned. You knew where you were going. That restaurant has a website with a menu listed. That restaurant also has a phone line. When my private clients know they have to eat out and they have no idea what to do, I will get on the phone to the restaurant and actually talk to the manager for them. (Yes, really.) I will find out what the best choice is for them *before they go*. And I will tell them how to log it. If they need a special accommodation, like please steam the broccoli and put the sauce on the side, just about every food establishment I talk to is happy to help. (Especially because I'm giving them advance warning.)

If you know you're going out, or it's someone's birthday, or you have to attend a potluck dinner, pre-planning and pre-logging your food is even more essential! You can adjust what you eat earlier in the day to stay within your macro percentages. Or you can look at a menu ahead of time and decide what you're going to eat hours before you get there. When you do that, you have complete control. You are much less likely to throw caution to the wind, cave in, and partake of that pitcher of margaritas your friends are sharing.

Logging your food *before* you eat will completely change your life. It gives you conscious control over what you're putting in your mouth. Your brain already knows what you're eating all day long, so it's less likely to try and steer you off track. And you have the opportunity to troubleshoot the tricky days before they get away from you.

You will no longer have to fear getting on the scale in the morning. If you tracked everything, followed the rules, and stayed within your parameters, you're all good.

RULE #6: **For heaven's sake, don't keep junk food in your house!**

You need to set yourself up to succeed. And if there's ice cream or cookies (or for me, Ritz crackers) anywhere in the house, you're going to cave in and eat them at some point. You might be able to resist once or twice, but sooner or later, that willpower is going to let you down.

Rebels live in a safe zone. That means cleaning out your cupboards, your refrigerator, your freezer, your "secret snack stash" in the car—everything! All the sugar. All the starchy carbs. All the alcohol. If you can't eat it on the program, get it out of your environment.

Now, I realize you may not live alone. And your family may not be on board with your new lifestyle (yet). So what do you do if your spouse simply *must* have cold beer in the fridge? Or your kids can't live without their afternoon snacks? There are solutions.

The first thing you need to do is explain to them that you are serious about this new lifestyle, and you need their help and support. You'll be amazed how helpful your family can be when you just ask. Then build some strategies and work-arounds.

If your husband needs that cold beer, consider getting him a mini-fridge and keeping it in the garage. If it's a huge temptation for you, have him put a padlock on the door. I'm totally serious! That's not weird. It's smart. Maybe your kids could eat their snacks at a friend's house, or you could stop for a treat on the way home from school. The whole idea is that your home is safe. There's no temptation there.

Do you always grab a doughnut and coffee when you stop to get gas? Have your husband keep the tank full for you. Or pay the extra two cents to go to a full-service gas station so you don't have to get out of the car. There's always a way to avoid the temptations. Get creative!

Okay, so what about when it's a holiday or special occasion? Same deal. No junk in the house. If you're hosting a party and there's tempting food there, fine. But the leftovers either go home with the guests or in the trash! If well-meaning friends drop by with a container of cookies, you don't have to insult them by refusing the gift. But get it out of the house as soon as they leave. Give it away. Take it to work. Or just throw it in the trash.

THIS IS YOUR LIFE. YOU ARE THE BOSS. If there's no junk in the house, you don't have to wrestle with your willpower. You'll be just fine.

RULE #7: Follow the Foods to Eat/Foods to Avoid list.

Here's where the rubber meets the road, my friend. This is where your decision to take your life back really begins. There's no way around it. You will have to give up some kinds of food—at least during weight-loss mode. Ideally, some of these things will never make it back into your diet, but for now they are definitely off-limits. Rather than listing 10 pages of individual foods, I'm going to group most of the foods into categories—like no grains, no alcohol, no cheese, etc.

The best way to succeed with this is to **KEEP IT SIMPLE**! Remember, you have to measure and weigh everything that goes into your mouth. You have to keep track of it all. And several major categories of food will not be allowed. So the fewer ingredients in a meal, the better. It's much easier to weigh and log a plain hamburger with lettuce, tomato, and no bun than it is to figure out what's in an "approved" shepherd's pie. Complicated recipes with lots of ingredients are just difficult. So stick with meat, eggs, vegetables, nuts, seeds, and fat. Make it easy on yourself.

If there's a food you're considering eating, and you're not sure if it's on the approved list, ask yourself two questions:

■ How much sugar does it have?

■ Does it have enough fat to keep me full?

If it's low-sugar and has a good amount of fat (or you can add fat to it), then it's probaby fine. If it's high in sugar, don't eat it!

I'm the kind of person who could just eat tuna out of a can every day for a month and be totally fine. But you're not me. If you need lots of variety, that's great. Just keep a list of meals you love, and rotate them in often. If you log a meal in Lose It once, it's stored forever. Use the tools available to you.

I've made a printable chart for you that's available in the resources section of my website. It lists all the foods to eat and foods to avoid. Print it out and post it where you will refer to it often. For now, here's the list.

WHAT DO I EAT?

OKAY TO EAT	AVOID THESE
👍 **Berries** (blackberries, blueberries, raspberries, strawberries)	👎 **Alcohol**
👍 **Eggs**	👎 **Cheese**
👍 **Full-fat cottage cheese**	👎 **Fruit** (other than the berries listed)
👍 **Full-fat, plain Greek traditional yogurt**	👎 **Grains** (including corn, oatmeal, quinoa, rice)
👍 **Healthy Fats** (avocado, butter, coconut oil, olive oil)	👎 **Juice**
👍 **Meat** (any)	👎 **Lentils/Legumes** (including peanuts/peanut butter)
👍 **Nuts & Seeds**	👎 **Pasta**
👍 **Seafood**	👎 **Potatoes**
👍 **Vegetables** (any)	👎 **Processed food**
	👎 **Soda**
	👎 **Sugar**
	👎 **Sweet potatoes**
	👎 **Yams**

13 Frequently Asked Questions

EVEN THOUGH THE RULES ARE AS STRAIGHTFORWARD as I can make them, questions will naturally pop up. So let's take a look at the ones I hear most often.

What If I'm Diabetic?

Let's talk a little bit about diabetes. It is a rampant disease and one we need to mention. In fact, a lot of people working toward better health have pre-diabetes or maybe even type I or II diabetes.

If you have pre-diabetes, that means your blood sugar is running higher than normal. Normal blood sugar is anywhere between 80 and 120, and pre-diabetes is when you find your blood sugars constantly higher than that. The good news for folks with pre-diabetes is that you can reverse it. And of course you want to reverse it, because diabetes is considered a terminal disease.

Most people think, "Well sure, I eat a chocolate chip cookie, and my blood sugar goes up." While that is true, it doesn't cover everything you need to know about how your blood sugar works. In a nutshell, when you eat something that causes your blood sugar to rise, your pancreas releases insulin, which brings your blood sugar levels back to normal. Diabetes is when your pancreas doesn't do this. Constant elevated blood sugar causes lots of problems, and if left uncorrected, it can kill you.

For folks with type I diabetes, in most cases they were born with a pancreas that doesn't make insulin. Through no fault of their own, their bodies don't produce what they need to bring their blood sugar down.

However, for folks with type II diabetes, their pancreas has been pumping out that insulin for so long that it just quits. Oftentimes, their pancreas is still secreting insulin, but at that point it is not enough to control their blood sugar without assistance. That assistance probably comes in the form of medications like Glucophage, or Metformin, and often insulin injections as well. Even in type II, people are not without hope. There is always hope, and making changes to diet and lifestyle can help people with type II control their blood sugars.

The main cause for this is the foods people eat. For example, it's not just chocolate chip cookies, or sweets in general, that cause your blood sugar to rise. Whenever people are eating a lot of sugar or carbs, their blood sugar is surging constantly, and the human pancreas can't keep producing that insulin forever. Eventually, it's like "I'm out, I can't do this anymore." Unchecked high blood sugar levels can lead to coma and death, so diabetes is a serious matter.

Too often people think, "Well, I just won't eat cookies anymore." That is all well and good, but what they don't know is that English muffin they enjoy every morning causes their blood sugar to rise just as much as any cookie they might eat. The fact that so few people realize is that carbs convert directly to sugar in your bloodstream. So you can claim you're on a "no-sugar diet," but if you're eating a morning bagel or a muffin instead, then that "diet" is bullcrap.

So for people with pre-diabetes, or types I or II, I recommend pulling anything that triggers an insulin response out of their diets. That's bread, any grains, oatmeal, pasta, potatoes, sweet potatoes, and yams. Remember that carbs are sugar, so that croissant is just as bad as a candy bar if you have diabetes.

The foods on your Okay to Eat list should not produce insulin responses. Insulin is an important hormone, but you don't want an abundance of it in your body. Think of insulin as the fat-producing hormone. You eat too much sugar, so the insulin comes along and stores it as fat to get it out of your blood. You don't want that.

How Often Should I Eat?

Our society has led us to believe that 3 meals and 2 snacks a day are neces-sary for our survival. Allow me to let you in on a little secret: We don't need to eat all the time.

Here's why people find themselves eating all day long. They wake up and have a bagel or some toast for breakfast. That causes their blood sugar to spike, and then they're hungry. They may need to medicate or take insulin to bring it down. But then, their blood sugar drops, so they eat some crackers or a muffin to bring it back up, where it spikes again.

This is not a personal attack on diabetics; this is the trap I want you all to avoid. These highs and lows are most often caused by eating the wrong foods.

Don't let fewer meals scare you. One of my clients shared with me that her husband has struggled with his blood sugar since Vietnam ended. For 40 years, his doctor has been on his case about high blood sugar. By follow-ing my program, he has finally been able to get his pre-diabetic state under control. By changing how he eats, he's avoided having to control his blood sugar through medication. This way of eating saved his life, literally.

Do not be afraid of limiting your intake to two or three meals a day. If you are eating the right things, you will not experience the typical spike and drop in your blood sugar. Some Rebels are perfectly happy with just one solid meal a day. By maintaining normal blood sugar levels, you will not have to eat constantly. When you give your body what it actually needs, when you feed your body the right things, you can start to trust it.

Everyone has heard "Breakfast is the most important meal of the day." However, if you're not hungry when you wake up, then don't eat. Guys, don't eat if you're not hungry! Don't force yourself to eat, that's a great way to get fat.

How Do I Avoid Sugar Spikes?

As I mentioned, certain foods will cause your blood sugar to spike. Sugary treats, fruits, carbs, grains, (especially refined grains like white bread), will all trigger an insulin response. Think about a plate of pancakes with maple syrup. That's pure sugar as far as your body is concerned. If you're trying to lose weight or if you're diabetic, that should not be your breakfast. If you must indulge, make sure to get some protein with that meal to slow your body's absorption of the sugar.

There are foods that will not provoke a blood sugar spike, but should still be avoided if you are trying to lose weight. One of them is cheese. On the surface, cheese looks perfect: no carbs, no sugar. It is pure fat, and while it won't provoke an insulin response, it will stop you from losing weight. Potatoes and fruit pose a similar problem. Are they better than cake and bagels? Yes. But they will slow or stop your weight loss.

How many parents feed their kids waffles and fruit juice for breakfast before packing them off to school? Those kids just got a major sugar spike, so they'll be hyper until about ten o'clock, and then they'll crash. Everyone thinks fruit juice is healthy, because Americans have been lied to for 40 years. Fruit juice is all the sugar (and oftentimes even more) of a piece of fruit with virtually none of the fiber. Once again, that breakfast needs to be eaten with protein to slow the absorption of all that sugar. If you are diabetic or trying to lose weight, fruit juice, waffles, cereal, and French toast should all be on your Don't Eat list.

What if I'm vegetarian? Can I still be a Code Red Rebel?

This is one of my favorite topics because so many people ask me whether the Code Red Lifestyle will work for vegans and vegetarians. The short answer is yes! But you will be more limited in your food options. Of course, vegetarians are used to that anyway because they voluntarily cut out some or all animal products.

I was vegan for a whole year from 2007–2008, and I know firsthand how it feels to live on just vegetables and grains. Let's just focus on vegetarians for the sake of argument. (You vegans are really great at figuring out how to modify your choices.)

If you're vegetarian, you're going to live on primarily vegetables and grains. I love vegetables and eat tons of them, even though I'm also adding in meat products. The big problem is the grains. Vegetarians tend to eat a lot of grains to fill themselves up. It's really hard to be satiated from just leafy greens and colorful veggies. So if you're a Code Red vegetarian, you've got to get lots of fat from natural sources. Fortunately, there are plenty of healthy plant-based fats like avocados, olives, nuts, seeds, coconut oil, and—if you eat them—eggs and fish, as well.

The fat will fill you up! Get used to eating lots of it!

You will have to give up the grains to thrive on this lifestyle. Grain-based bread, pasta, rice, crackers, cereals, and snack foods are fueling the painful inflammation in your body and keeping you from losing weight. The grains I'm talking about include barley, corn, millet, quinoa, rice, rye, and wheat. Technically some of these are seeds, and corn isn't really a grain, but these substances all raise inflammation levels in your body.

Another big staple in a vegetarian diet is starch. Foods like potatoes, sweet potatoes, yams, and such are bulky, but the starch will absolutely stop your weight loss. So while you're in weight-loss mode, avoid these. Once you're maintaining, you can add them back in a little at a time.

So what does that leave you with? Vegetables, nuts, seeds, eggs, fish, and plant-based fats and oils. Is it limited? Yeah, but so is any vegetarian diet. If you want to feel better and lose the weight, you've got to get rid of the grains.

Why Can I Eat _____, But Not _____?

Why can I eat berries, but not other fruit?

Why cottage cheese and cream cheese, but not cheddar?

Why vegetables, but not legumes?

Here's the deal—the goal is to lose weight, preferably as quickly as possible, right? There is nothing "wrong" with some of the foods on the Avoid list. Cheddar cheese has no sugar and no carbs, so it should be fine. Berries are a fruit, so why can't we have peaches? The reason is that these foods will stall your weight loss or even cause you to gain weight. Even though they may be perfectly healthy, you should not eat them while you're in weight-loss mode.

It doesn't seem fair, I get it. The best advice I can give you is to just accept the "Do Not Eat" list and lose the weight as quickly as possible! Weight-loss mode does not last forever. Even if you have over 100 pounds to lose, doing it the Code Red way will get it off you faster than you ever thought possible. There will come a time when you will be able to add those peaches back in, or the cheese, or the hummus and lentils. But for now, trust me and keep them off your plate.

STAYING POWER: STICKING TO YOUR NEW WAY OF THINKING

Let's talk about staying motivated.

The time of year when people are most motivated is New Year's Day, right? So many people make those whole-hearted resolutions. But let's face it, after the ball drops, a lot of people drop their motivation too.

I promise you can stick with a diet for the first 2 weeks of the new year. I know you can hit the gym 5 times a week...for the first 2 weeks. But how do you keep going long after you feel like doing it? How do you stay motivated? Here are 3 tips for staying motivated long after those fuzzy feelings are gone—no matter what time of year it is.

1.   **CLEAN OUT YOUR NEWSFEED.** No matter how you spin it, social media is a part of our lives. We're on our favorite platforms continuously. So get rid of the crap that doesn't line up with your new way of thinking. For example, if you're trying to cut back on wine, stop following sites that talk about wine. You know what I mean—advertisements, or worse, friends' posts that say things like "It's wine-thirty" or "I need a glass of wine" or "Who wants to meet up for a glass of wine?"

     You don't need that feeding into your thoughts. If you're trying to cut back on eating sweets, you don't need a bunch of dessert recipes in your newsfeed. You don't need to read posts about how to bake the perfect chocolate cake or Grandma's chocolate chip cookies. Cleaning out your newsfeed will help you clean out your body and your mind.

2. **HANG OUT WITH LIKE-MINDED PEOPLE.** The old saying goes, "Show me your friends, and I'll show you your future." That's exactly right. If you're trying to get really fit, and you want to look like the super-lean CrossFit people, then you should hang out with CrossFit people. Find people who, like you, are motivated to get to bed early so they can wake up for their 5:00 a.m. workout. Go to breakfast with them, have coffee with them. Spend time absorbing their mindsets and habits. Hang out with people that are like-minded, and avoid people who don't align with your new way of thinking.

3. **BUY SOME HIGH-QUALITY CLOTHES THAT FIT.** It sounds kind of simple, I know, but go out and get some good-quality, nice-fitting clothes. As you lose weight, your jeans will get droopy and start to fall off. Your shirts will start to look like dresses. And at first, you'll be excited. It means you're making progress. But you'll quickly find that those baggy clothes just make you feel frumpy. Loose pants can even make you feel like you could eat a little more. When your clothes fit properly, you feel amazing! People notice your progress. And you're less likely to stray off the plan when you know how awesome you look.

If you're worried about having to replace your whole wardrobe every few weeks (yes, it does happen that fast), you can always shop at thrift stores. Or do a clothing swap with a friend who is just a little bit ahead of you. You don't have to spend a lot of money, but the investment is so worth it. You're worth it!

Michele McTiernan-Gleason

Lost 40 Pounds and Learned to Care For Herself—Body, Mind, and Spirit

I HAVE BEEN a nurturing, caring person to the people around me since I was 10 years old. All through my life, I have focused my attention on the care of others before myself.

My husband, a navy veteran, was in an accident that left him disabled for life. After his accident, the doctors told me that he would only recover to a certain point, and that he would never be the same again. In addition, my son was also in an automobile accident. So before I even began my weight-loss journey, my husband and son were in hospital beds in the house, requiring round-the-clock care for several years. I consider myself so blessed to have them in my life.

As I cared for my husband, and as my son eventually recovered, I was looking after everyone but myself. I didn't give myself the same love and compassion that I gave others, and by doing that, I let myself get into what I call the crazy train of the chronic stress cycle. I was in a Catch-22. My adrenals were fatigued, which caused me to gain weight, and then because of the excess weight, my adrenals were fatigued even more.

Because I was caring for my husband and son as well as working, I began to experience odd symptoms myself. I went to various doctors for three years, but all they said was that the symptoms were related to stress. I was having problems with clarity, and honestly, I just didn't feel right. I *knew* something was wrong.

I am a dedicated student of clinical science and medicine. I went to nursing school and studied applied science. So one day, I woke up and decided to figure out what was wrong with me. I sat down

was wrong. I believe in a full life balance—spiritual, emotional, and physical well-being. And I could tell my body was out of sync.

As it happened, I was at the grocery store when they called with the results. "We're really sorry to tell you this, but you have a very large brain tumor on your right frontal lobe, and we need you to come in right away."

After we spoke about my history, she said to me, "I am going to walk this journey with you, by your side, 24 hours a day, 7 days a week, day and night. I won't let you down, and I'll be with you until you reach your goals."

with a notepad and listed every symptom I could remember experiencing over the last three years, no matter how minute. Within an hour, I determined that it was neurological, and I suspected I had multiple sclerosis.

I took my findings to the doctor and requested an MRI. The doctors were skeptical, and probably thought I was crazy, but I just *knew* something

As I continued shopping, I told them that I had too much to do, I was taking care of my husband, and I was finishing up a degree program and wanted to be able to walk at commencement. They told me that was not an option, and that I needed immediate attention. I was shocked. *Three years* I had been to doctors who told me there was absolutely nothing wrong with me.

I finished shopping, went out to the car, and prepared my husband. "I have some *really* bad news to tell you, but you have to promise not to get upset." I told him, and he handled it really well. I just told him that I was going to take care of this, like I do, and that everything would be alright. I spent the next 48 hours getting my affairs in order. While it was decided that they would perform brain surgery, I had no idea whether I would survive.

My surgeon was a retired army doctor, recently back in the states from the Middle East, a really gifted, talented surgeon. He was able to remove most of the tumor, and in 7 years, it has not come back. Even though I live with the possibility of that tumor growing back or taking my life, it has been my greatest blessing. That tumor was a sign showing me I had been neglecting my own physical health.

HOW CRISTY SAVED MY LIFE

Even with all of my research and education in health, physiology, and integrated medicine, I was never able to get my own weight off. I was eating healthy food, but I couldn't understand why the weight stayed with me. I didn't eat sugar, didn't eat inflammatory food. I ate whole foods, with lots of complex carbs. All I could think was *What am I doing wrong?*

I met Cristy through a professional network here in Idaho, and was immediately impressed with her outlook and her demeanor. I've never met a more authentic and balanced person. She is strong, direct, and confident, but also soft and compassionate. We shared the same understanding about the right way to live in terms of nutrition. Most of all, I was impressed with her belief in the importance of whole person care—mind, body, and spirit.

As a life-long caregiver, hearing those words struck me like none ever have. Hearing words that no one in my life has ever said to me brought tears to my eyes and peace to my spirit. I knew then that she was different, and that she was going to stick by me through anything.

I learned I was eating too many carbs. Even though they were complex, whole food carbs, I was getting too much. I also learned that I was eating too frequently throughout the day. Finally, I wasn't weighing or measuring my food, and if you want to lose weight, you have to track it. Cristy says, "What gets weighed and measured gets managed."

My biggest challenge was feeling hungry at night. My calorie intake was limited anyway because I am a small person, so not snacking at night or eating after 6:30 was an adjustment. But on the program, I was eating food that I loved like sour cream, cream cheese, bacon, and guacamole. I hadn't been eating sugar anyway, so I did not have to deal with sugar detox.

I lost 40 pounds in 90 days. I credit my belief in mind and spirit for the relative ease of my weight loss. I needed Cristy's loving support and encouragement, as well as the right tools to lose weight. Once I had my own progress dialed in, I

was able to reach out to the other Rebels and provide extra emotional and spiritual support, which is so important to the healing process.

Our country's focus right now is on wealth over health, and that mentality leads to the kind of pandemic of obesity and diabetes we see today. Let me tell you, when you are the truth giver, you can be subject to a lot of ridicule. What we do with Cristy currently goes against the commonly accepted norms for nutrition, and people struggle to accept and support what goes against their beliefs. But as Rebels, we are true to ourselves and to each other. We *know* the Code Red Rebel Lifestyle *works* and is revolutionizing the field of nutrition.

If you are planning to start living the Code Red Lifestyle, listen to Cristy and implement every aspect of the program. Whatever you were doing before this point obviously wasn't working, so go all in, and don't underestimate the importance of your spiritual and emotional well-being. It's all interconnected.

14 Weight-Loss Mode

HERE WE GO! Weight-loss mode is a state of mind for Code Red Rebels. It's where you stick to your guns, no matter what. Christmas, birthdays, deaths in the family—none of these matter. You find other ways to celebrate and deal with stress. Weight-loss mode is where you get to stand in your power. You have the power and you have the control to handle this. Trust me, you do!

This isn't some quick-fix 30-day plan. You stay in weight-loss mode until you reach your goal weight. For some people, it might be 30 days. For others, it might be several months. But if you stay strong and rely on the Code Red community for support, it will take a lot less time than you might think. Every person is different, but I have private clients who lose ½ to 1 pound a day with no trouble. And they are healthy!

Remember, you're in charge of how fast and how long your body is using fat for fuel. If you cheat once, you've switched your body back to sugar, and it can take up to a week switch it back over. Stay strong.

You're Not Going to Starve

Over the course of your weight-loss program, you will gradually consume fewer and fewer calories. You might be surprised by this, but in today's society, people need a lot fewer calories than they think.

I know that sounds like bad news. If you're used to eating 5,000 calories a day, the idea of dropping it down that far is scary. The good news, though, is you will lose weight. If your body is used to 3,000 calories, then it will naturally lose weight when you cut that number down and give it the right foods. As you lose weight, you are going to eat less, and that is okay, because your body changes as you lose weight.

In the first week, you're going to eat a lot of calories. Guaranteed. It's a natural reaction, because your body is getting used to a new way to eat and it's hungry. Often, in week two, people notice a natural decrease in intake. I'll hear things like Wow. You know, I had budgeted myself two eggs and four strips of bacon, but I only had one egg and three strips." That is a sign of someone naturally feeling less hungry. That's good. Forget the clean-plate club. Never force yourself to eat if you're not hungry.

My mom doesn't like to eat breakfast. She has just never been very hungry in the morning, so she doesn't eat until 11 a.m., and then she's good until about 5 p.m. Personally, I like to skip dinner. I'll have breakfast and lunch, but I find that I don't really need to eat dinner. There is no cookie cutter method. Everyone is going to eat their meals differently. But the fact is, you will eat less as you adjust to this program. Don't force calories.

If you're into weeks 3 and 4, and the weight is not coming off, it typically means you're forcing yourself to eat more calories. Most people will naturally start to eat less, but sometimes I need to tell people it's okay not to eat the full amount all the time. The rule of thumb is this: If you're not hungry, don't eat.

Sometimes people ask me, "But Cristy, what about starvation mode? Won't I tank my metabolism if I eat fewer than 1,200 calories? Won't my body start holding onto fat if I don't eat 6 times a day?" They are genuinely scared that their bodies will shut down and not lose weight if they don't eat that magical 1,200 calories.

First of all, everyone has a different number of calories they need to survive based on their age, weight, activity level, and basal metabolic rate. That's the reason that I have to calculate precise numbers of calories and fat/carb/protein ratios for every private client. There's no magic number that works for everyone.

The whole starvation mode idea, and the notion that you need to eat 6 times a day, these are more lies we've been told by the food industry. Think about it. Who benefits when we eat more food? Umm...the people selling us that food! The truth is you probably don't need that many calories. You need energy. But when you're eating high-fat, healthy foods like avocado, you get twice as much energy and nutrition per gram of food. Which means you don't need the same volume as when you were eating sugar and simple carbs. Your brain may want to eat more. Your eyeballs might miss the big plates overflowing with mashed potatoes and gravy. Your *emotions* might want dessert. But your physical body doesn't need it to survive.

If you're *really* low on calories, like 500 a day for 30 days straight, then yes, you could possibly damage your metabolism. But if you're truly listening to your body and feeding it real food, it's unlikely you'll get to that point. Your body knows what it needs. And if you're overweight, then it needs to burn off all that extra energy you've been storing as fat. The more calories you eat, the fewer your body needs to pull from the fat reserves.

The best way to judge where you should be is to listen to your body. Are you actually hungry? If so, eat a high-fat meal. If you're not, don't eat.

What Should I Expect the First Week?

The first week is gonna be hard. I'm not going to lie to you (ever). When you've been eating a standard Western diet full of sugars and grains and caffeine and chemicals, you body needs to detox all that crap out of your system. And it ain't gonna be pretty. But don't let that scare you, because you are strong and you can get through it! I think it helps to know what to expect, but realize that it's different for every person. Not everyone experiences this stuff, and you might get through the first week without a problem.

Here's the thing—sugar is 8 times more addictive than cocaine. So depending on how much sugar you've been consuming and how hooked you are on those sodas and snacks, you can expect your withdrawal symptoms to be similar to withdrawing from narcotics. You might experience headaches, nausea, shaking, achy joints, a foggy head, and/or extreme fatigue. You might be so exhausted you can't function at all.

Many people describe detoxing from sugar and grains as having flu-like symptoms. You're going to be hungry and grumpy. Little things might start to bother you. If you've been consuming 4 or 5 sugary sodas a day and you switch to plain water, of course you're going to feel like crap for a little while. The symptoms can last just a few days or up to a week or more.

Most people tell me that around Day 8, they feel like a veil has lifted, revealing a whole new level of energy and clarity that they didn't know was possible. They feel better than they have in years, maybe decades. The headaches and stiffness go away. They think clearly. And **THEY JUST FEEL GOOD**! Everyone I've watched go through this says it was totally worth toughing it out through that first week to get to the amazing feeling on the other side.

So as you start feeling those withdrawal symptoms, don't quit! Take it easy on yourself. Don't make any big plans. If you can stay home for a few days, that will help. And it is 100% okay to take over-the-counter pain relievers for your headaches just to get you through.

Remember, this short-term discomfort is going to pay off big-time! You are strong, Rebel. I believe in you.

What's the Deal with Detox?

You might have heard all sorts of talk about detoxing. It's all part of the fad diet marketing frenzy. Many people come to me confused about detoxing. There's so much mixed information out there, and they don't know what to believe. And I totally get it. It's incredibly confusing. A lot of that information is designed to sell you something. So let me just break it down into simple language.

Your body already knows how to detox itself. It knows how to completely heal and cleanse itself. It just needs a few basic things from you. First of all, it needs a lot of water. I'm not talking about LaCroix or sugar-free Crystal Light or beverages made with water. No. Just plain old water with maybe some lemon or lime added for flavor. Give your body lots of water, and it will naturally flush your system of any toxicity.

SHOULD YOU TAKE SUPPLEMENTS?

Why is something as important as vitamins and minerals so controversial? Some people say you absolutely need to take supplements, and to buy their very expensive brand. Others say you get enough from your food, and not to worry about it.

My opinion falls somewhere in the middle. When you eat real food, you will be consuming a good portion of the vitamins and minerals you need to survive. But depending on where you live, and where your food comes from, there may be more or less nutrition in that head of broccoli.

For one thing, the soil in certain areas has been depleted of its natural ability to supply nutrients to plants. Another consideration is how long that food has been making its way to you. If you can go out back, pick your own food from a garden, and cook it within 10 minutes, you're getting the maximum nutrition that soil can provide. If you buy fresh produce in the grocery store, it may have been picked weeks ago. In that case, frozen produce can actually have more nutrition than the fresh stuff.

So what do you really need?

Your body will cleanse itself. It will heal itself. It can do that.

Now, it only makes sense that if you're trying to "reset" and rid your body of toxins, you can't be adding new ones in at the same time, right? You can't cleanse or detox and still be drinking beer at night, you know what I'm saying? It's counterproductive. Eating a doughnut on the way to work? Not gonna help. Even starting your morning off with Raisin Bran. You're just giving your body extra work to do. Your body can handle itself, as long as you're not creating this perpetual cycle of crap.

It's a good idea to check with your medical professional and maybe even get some bloodwork done, if you think you might be vitamin deficient. But as far as the Code Red Lifestyle goes, you're definitely going to want to supplement vitamin D3 and magnesium. It's a rare case when someone is not highly deficient in these two.

When you eat a high-fat, low-carb diet, your body will flush out the electrolytes you need to keep vital functions going. When you're low on these electrolytes, especially magnesium, it will often show up as muscle cramps. If that happens to you, don't panic. The magnesium will help. You also may want to salt your food, as sodium flushes out at a higher rate with this lifestyle.

I learned something interesting after getting my own bloodwork done. My nurse practitioner said, "I thought you were taking vitamin D?" I was taking 5,000 units every day. Then she said, "Well, it's not even showing up in your bloodwork." We discovered that I was taking a low-quality brand and was only absorbing about 30% of the dose. So we switched to a high-quality brand, and I now get a 70% absorption rate. So make sure you're using a good-quality supplement. I use the Pure Encapsulation brand. But you can ask your doctor what they recommend.

Once you've got the garbage out of your system—you've detoxed all the chemicals and sugar and your system is squeaky clean—then what? Are you going to go right back to the doughnuts and coffee? It's no wonder people's systems burn out and become diseased.

Yes, it's worth the work to detox your body.

No, you don't need to buy anything to help it.

Just eat clean. Drink water. And don't mess it up when you're done.

Don't fall for the advertising about detoxing shakes or pills or powders. Your body knows how to take care of itself. It just needs a little bit of help from you, okay?

I Can, But I Don't Want To

Recently, I was at a two-day conference, and one of the treats they served was Rice Krispie bars. Let me tell you, I love Rice Krispie bars! I really do. But at this particular conference, I didn't have any. There was no willpower involved. I just didn't want them.

People ask me questions about my program all the time, and one of the ones I hear most often is "When can I eat the foods I want? When can I cheat? You know, when can I have the pizza? When can I have the Rice Krispie bars? When can I have the ice cream?"

The first thing I try to clarify is what exactly they're asking. If they're asking when they can "cheat," the answer is it depends on their goals. Are they in weight-loss mode? Then they can't have the ice cream or the pizza or whatever until they reach their goal weight. If they're already at their goal and just trying to maintain and live a healthy lifestyle, then I guess they can have it occasionally.

But they're missing the point.

When you eat real food, without all the added sugar and chemicals, your mind switches to where you don't want that crap anymore. I didn't turn down the Rice Krispie bar because I had to or because everybody was watching. I didn't eat it because I didn't want to.

I didn't want to.

I finally got myself to the point where I wasn't craving it. I wasn't thinking about it at all. And it wasn't an agonizing decision. It was a total non-issue.

That's what I want for you.

I want you to get to the point where you can, but you just don't want to.

Do I eat foods that aren't great for me? Sure. Once in a great while. My husband, Miles, and I go out for a date night once a month. But we don't eat out unless it's date night. It's just a lifestyle we've developed. We'd rather eat in.

And you know what? It physically *hurts* me when I eat crap. It hurts my tummy. And it's a slippery slope when I eat carbs and sugar. It makes me crave more carbs and sugar, and I just don't want to go down that path again. At all. I've been heavy before. I don't ever want to go back there. I don't want to because getting six-pack abs means more to me. Not feeling sick all night means more to me.

You might not care about having six-pack abs. Maybe you just want to get off prescription medication. Or you want your skin to clear up. Or you just want to play outside with your kids without feeling like you're gonna have a heart attack. You get to decide that those things mean more than a bowl of ice cream or half a pizza.

You are worth more than that. You deserve more than that.

Treat yourself like royalty. Feed your body and soul only the very best. Because you deserve it.

It all starts in the mind. You have to **DECIDE YOU'RE WORTH IT**.

Then after a while, your body falls in line.

It's a little like magic. When you stop eating carbs and sugar. When you stop putting chemicals into your body. You get used to it. Your body stops craving the junk and starts craving the good stuff.

I get it. The year has a seemingly endless flow of food-based celebrations. Birthday parties, retirement parties, weddings. The list goes on. And we've been trained since we were children to eat crap food at all of these occasions. I'm not telling you that you *can't* have those things. I'm offering you a choice. If you stick with me, eventually you will come to a point where you don't want them.

The less you eat the crap. The less you'll want it.

In the short term, get into the habit of talking to yourself before you eat or drink anything. (You can do it silently, so people don't look at you funny.) When you get home after a long day of shopping and you just want to order a pizza, or when you're at that party and you're faced with sugary cocktails or cheese and crackers, say this:

> I can have that _____ if I really want it.
>
> Right now, my body feels _____.
>
> If I decide to eat/drink that, my body will feel _____.
>
> Tomorrow morning, I will feel _____.
>
> Do I really want it?

Then make a decision. And let me give you a hint. We all have different voices. Chances are, there's a big voice that says, "It's a special occasion. Go ahead—eat it!"

If you really pay attention, there's probably also a smaller voice. One that's quietly saying, "The last time you ate that, you were sick all night. Remember? Your stomach was cramping and you felt like crap the next day. Maybe it's best to skip it." Or maybe it's saying, "But you promised this year would be different..."

The rest of this book will give you strategies and tactics to "survive" those work conferences or parties and all the food, drink, and stress they bring, without gaining 10 pounds. The cool thing is that if you follow these strategies, chances are pretty good that you'll be able to attend all the special occasions you like, already adapted, and without the fear of gorging on cake. You'll be amazed how much easier it will be to say "I don't want it" every day after that.

Listen to the little voice. It's smart. It's you.

The more you listen to it, the louder and bolder it will grow.

You can have it. But you don't have to want it.

Your choice.

You Won't Have to Weigh and Measure Forever

It is a big change. We have all chosen to commit to a life of health, and we have chosen to honor our bodies by providing them with wholesome, nutritious food. Logging every ounce of that healthy food, weighing and measuring every gram of fat and protein are a huge change from the way you used to eat before your commitment to health. So take encouragement from this when I tell you, you will not always have to weigh and measure everything.

The weight-loss phase is the hardest part. I am on your case about every-thing, and you push as hard as you can to get to your goal weight. I ask my clients if they're leveling their measuring spoons, if they are pre-logging their food. I ask my clients if they're staying on top of their water. I know how hard it is to weigh and measure everything you consume, but it is the only way to keep track of your success in the weight-loss phase of this program.

While you are focused on that, make yourself aware of the positive changes occurring in your body. Your blood pressure starts to come down. Your cholesterol starts to decrease. Folks who are in a pre-diabetic state begin to lose that status. Your clothes will start to fit better. There are so many other ways to measure good health, and we count every one of them as a victory. You still get on that scale every day, but if the dial doesn't move as much as you hoped it would, remember the other benefits of your efforts.

The time is coming where your body will reliably know what it needs, and you won't have to put everything on the food scale anymore. Your body will tell you when it's hungry and when it isn't. You will know the difference between hun-ger and thirst. When that time comes, you can eat to your comfort level.

I have weighed 154 pounds for 16 years, and I know that because I get on the scale every day. The scale is your first line of defense. If you put 2 pounds on one week, you should know why. You don't want months to go by with-out getting on the scale and suddenly you're 8, 12, 20 pounds up from your goal weight.

Once you are at your goal weight, you will no longer need to put all your food on a scale. You won't have to keep measuring spoons in your purse anymore. You have worked so hard to lose weight; maintaining your goal weight is the prize. That is the hope, or the light at the end of the tunnel. You can never go back to eating the way you did before you made your commitment to good health, but you won't always have to weigh and measure everything either. In fact, on maintenance there are only 3 non-negotiable rules:

Keep drinking one gallon of water a day.

Keep weighing yourself every morning.

Keep the junk food out of your house.

Troubleshooting

What if you're doing everything right, but you're not losing weight? First of all, realize that when you weigh yourself every day, it's easy to think 3 or 4 days with no weight loss is a stall. But technically a stall is when you have a couple of weeks with no progress. So cut yourself some slack. Sometimes your body just needs to catch up with your losses so far.

How long should you wait before diagnosing a weight gain?

1st day > Let it go.

2nd day > Start asking questions.

3rd day > It's time to figure it out.

Here's how to figure out what's going on with your body. Just ask yourself these questions:

DID YOU GET ENOUGH SLEEP? Your body will not let go of fat if you're not getting enough sleep.

DID YOU DRINK ALL YOUR WATER? Ice cubes don't count; you can't measure them. You really do need to drink that gallon every day. It makes a difference.

ARE YOU MEASURING ACCURATELY, OR ARE YOU EYE-BALLING IT? Do not free-pour the cream into your coffee. A heaping teaspoon is not a teaspoon—you have to level it off. Sloppy measuring is often the cause of a gain or a stall.

Sometimes You Do Everything Right and Still Get Stuck

It happens to everybody at some point. Say you have been drinking your water, avoiding the foods from the Do Not Eat list, keeping your sugars and carbs low, and getting your sleep. You're doing everything you need to do, but you hop on the scale and it doesn't budge. It's frustrating, I know. This is not the time to give up. If you stick to the program, that needle *will* move. If you are doing what you need to do, the weight *will* come off.

If your basal metabolic rate is 2,000 calories a day and you are eating 1,500 calories a day, it is physiologically impossible for your weight not to drop off. The last thing I want you to do is worry because the scale hasn't dropped. The scale isn't the only metric you can use to track your progress. Because if you are eating the right things, drinking your water, and getting enough sleep, you're healing your body from the inside. Losing weight isn't the only result of your efforts. There is so much more going on than what shows up on the scale.

You're getting your energy back. Your skin and nails are finally getting what they need to grow and shine. Your cholesterol is going down. If you're working your way out of a diabetic or pre-diabetic state, your body is working hard to repair itself. Even when the scale isn't going down, you probably notice that your clothes fit better, or are starting to feel a little loose. So trust the system. If the scale freezes, it doesn't mean that you're not still improving your health. That weight *will* begin to drop off again.

If my clients are stuck at the same weight for two weeks, then we'll talk about it. We'll want to talk about some of the different things that might be going on. It could be their body is taking that time to really repair itself, or maybe we need to think about changing some parts of the program to account for undiagnosed food sensitivities. Either way, if that scale gets stuck, don't panic, and whatever you do, **DON'T GIVE UP**.

Trust the system, and that scale will eventually start moving down again.

You Are Not the Problem; The Problem Is the Problem

Work the problem. It's not you. That might seem confusing, but I want you to stop beating yourself up when things don't go perfectly. I'll give you an example.

I have a client I have been working with for 2 ½ years. She bounces between success and regression. She will do awesome and lose 30 pounds, but then binge on her husband's junk food. Her husband, unfortunately, refuses to eat healthy and keeps his junk food in the house where it doesn't belong. So my client, who works so hard to avoid the temptation of bad food in her space every day, eventually breaks down.

What is so sad is that she thinks there is something wrong with her. She asks me, "What is wrong with me?" She says the junk food doesn't even taste good, but she shoves it down anyway. I asked her what she would do if the food wasn't in the cupboard. She said that if it wasn't in the house, she wouldn't eat it. *Ding ding ding*—we have a winner!

We talked about her options. She is 50% owner of that house, and 50% of that marriage. We talked about asking her husband to keep his junk food somewhere other than the cupboard. Whether it's in his man-cave, his office, the garage, wherever—if it is not in the space she uses, then she won't eat it.

So part of this process is identifying the problem. Instead of asking, "What's wrong with me?" or "Why am I so messed up?" focus on identifying the problem. For this client, it was simply a matter of moving her husband's junk food to a bin in a part of the house where she won't have to look at it every day. She already knew she could lose the weight, she just needed the garbage out of her space. This is working the problem. Take the focus and blame off yourself and put your energy into solving the actual issue. In this case, the problem was this lady had to stare junk food in the face every time she opened her cupboard. By removing that constant visual temptation, she eliminated the problem.

I have another client who is a high-powered 1% earner. She leads work conferences where she teaches people how to do their jobs. She finds that after these conferences, she binges. Again, her response is "Why do I do this? What's wrong with me?" Who cares about why? I don't care about why. I care about how to solve that problem. With this client, I learned that when she gets home from a conference, she is alone in the house and heads for the pantry.

There we can find the answer. She goes home. She doesn't go to the store, she doesn't order out. She goes to her space and raids her own cupboard. Here the issue is in two parts. On one hand, she had food in her house that she shouldn't. One of the three big rules is to keep unhealthy food out of your house, and this is why.

The other face of the problem, which she and I identified together, is that when she comes out of one of these big conferences, she's running at high energy. She can't go straight home or she will take that anxiety with her to the pantry. She found she needs to go to a hotel or somewhere she can be away from food until she comes down off that conference high.

It is up to you to fix your problems. If you want to see a counselor or a thera-pist to figure out why you have a problem, that's fine. I support that. However you need to identify and fix the problem first. Leave the "why" alone for now and just work the problem.

But do me and yourself a favor and don't put it all on you. No "Why me?" No "Why can't I change?" None of that. That is not going to help you push for-ward. The problem is what you need to figure out, not yourself. You are not the problem; the problem is the problem. The sooner you can identify the prob-lem, the sooner you can fix it and move forward.

How Will You Reward Yourself?

You're about to discover how rewarding it is to watch the dial on the scale tick down as you heal your life with real, nutritious food. That should make you feel awesome because it is a visible way to watch your progress in real time. Stepping on that scale is just as much a validation of your hard work as it is the first line of defense for keeping you on the right track. However, as wonderful as the weight loss is, it's important to remember that it's not all there is.

You are healing your body. You are healing your mind. There are countless invisible benefits you are achieving by feeding yourself the right food. Your A1C is going down, so those of you with pre-diabetic status get to wave good-bye to that designation. Remember, by eating those healthy fats, you guys are bringing your cholesterol down. That's why you're a Code Red Rebel. For over 40 years, you've been taught that fats give you high cholesterol, but that's not how it works. You're changing your thinking, and you're taking back your life.

Your body will not take long to get on board with eating the right way. As you feed yourself wholesome, nutritious food, you will begin to learn exactly what your body needs. You will know the difference between thirst and hunger. As your body heals, you will eventually be able to trust its cravings, because it will be craving what it needs. Your body will perform better, your skin will glow. Take that as your body's gratitude for you treating it better. That is the beauty of nutrition; it starts working right away. The sooner you feed your body healthy and wholesome food, the sooner you will begin to feel the rewards.

You care about your body. That is why you're giving it more sleep, more water, more sunshine, and more positive affirmation. Your mind needs all those things just as much as your body does. Get in front of that mirror and tell yourself, "You're beautiful." Tell yourself you're smart, you're strong. Tell yourself that you're getting healthier every day, and you're a good parent or boss. Whoever you are and whatever you do, affirm to yourself that you are good at it, because by healing your body, you are making your entire self better. You are making a difference.

So you are working very hard and transforming the way you eat and live. You are losing weight and healing your life. How will you reward yourself for all your hard work? My business coach clued me in to this concept. I worked so hard to build up my business, and my coach had me write out every year what

I was going to do to reward myself for reaching my goals. I planned clothes shopping for reaching my goals. What will you plan to reward yourself for reaching yours?

Now, a lot of you are parents, professionals, or caregivers. You're not used to thinking about giving to yourself, so you might be tempted to skip this. Don't! You are working so hard, and treating your body so well, you need to recognize that. The ultimate goal is always your health, but it is important to value your efforts as well. If someone in your life achieved a remarkable goal, you would reward them, so why not yourself?

You want to plan ahead, and sometimes that can be difficult because we all have busy lives. But your hard work is worth it. Obviously, you want to reward yourself with something other than food. Part of the wholesome change you have made in your life is to no longer punish or reward yourself with food. What are your interests? What makes you feel good? It could be going out and making some new additions to your wardrobe, or it could be a weekend at the spa. Maybe it's a pair of really nice noise-canceling headphones. I don't know what reward will feel the best for you, but you do.

For some people, it's taking a pair of jeans they used to feel really good in and hanging them up somewhere they can see them every day. Their goal is fitting into those jeans and feeling good in them again. Set some time aside to figure out what will be the most rewarding to you. You have worked so hard, so reward yourself, whether it's a weekend to go see a friend who lives far away, a new bicycle, dance lessons—whatever will help you feel good about your accomplishment.

Whatever it is, you want that reward to look forward to as well as your ultimate goal. Your body is healing and your health is improving, but when the scale isn't moving, people get frustrated. When that happens, look to your reward. It's a tangible thing to keep striving toward. I want you to keep working hard, I want you to feel encouraged and happy. And when you do reach your goal, I want you to reward yourself because, guess what?

You've earned it.

Pick Your Hard!

No matter how skilled you might be at playing soccer, there are times when it's challenging. No matter how beautifully you may play the piano, you put in long, difficult hours to learn. No matter how much you love your children, parenting is hard. Everything in life has moments where it's hard, sometimes a lot of moments in a row. And really, if life were always easy, it wouldn't mean much, would it?

I don't think anyone would argue with me that being obese is hard. You don't have to be on *The Biggest Loser* or *My 600-Pound Life* to be obese. If 30% of your body weight is fat, then you are obese. That means you don't have to weigh 300, 400, or 500 pounds to be in this category. If you weigh 250 pounds and 75 pounds of that is fat, you are obese. Obesity creates a host of other diseases and problems that nobody wants to deal with. Whether someone has diabetes, chronic joint pain, heart disease, or cancer, obesity is hard.

Sure you get to eat whatever you want, but your clothes don't fit. You feel like you're going to pass out after climbing a flight of stairs. You don't have the energy to run around in the backyard with your children or grandchildren. Your knees and back ache all the time. Or maybe you have no confidence because you hate the way you look. Or you don't like having sex with your spouse because you don't want to take your clothes off. Obesity is a rough place to be, and that is why everyone wants out.

On the flip side, weight loss and real nutrition are tough, too. My clients tell me that my program is hard. Being obese is hard, losing weight is hard, and maintaining a goal weight is hard, too.

You have to **PICK YOUR HARD**.

You can choose to be obese and stay in that abusive relationship with food, or you can transform your life with dedication and nutritious food. It's entirely up to you. But don't fool yourself—both options are hard.

It takes work to get fit. If you admire a swimmer's physique, or anyone with strong lean muscles, know that they have to work to keep that up. You see dancers or CrossFit people or runners—they all work hard and follow rules to look the way they do.

Any way you slice it, you will have to work at something. So my advice to you is to work hard to lose weight. Just make up your mind that you're going to do it, and tackle it head on.

What is it going to take? You're going to have to do these things:

- Plan your meals ahead.

- Pack approved, nutritional lunches and dinners.

- Measure out your portions.

- Get on the scale every day.

- Drink your water every day.

- Refuse to buy or bring home junk food.

- And, if you're on one of my personal programs, **YOU'RE GOING TO HAVE TO ANSWER TO ME IF YOU STRAY** outside the parameters I set for you.

These rules are non-negotiable. I don't care if you are flying to a conference in Las Vegas, you bring your food scale and your measuring spoons and make your own lunches there. I don't care if the company is providing lunches. If that provided lunch is not on your list, eat your own food during a break.

All change is hard. But this change, the commitment you make to improve your life and heal your body, it's a good change. It's the best change. And it's going to make the rest of your life so much easier!

I come from an obese family, and I have been heavy myself. I never want to deal with that again, so I work hard and follow the same rules I am asking you to follow. I have trained actors, models, and celebrities, and they had to follow the same rules too. No matter who you are, you have to work to maintain a certain weight and a certain physique.

The bottom line is that everything is hard and everything is easy. Avoiding cancer and heart disease is hard. Dancing at your grandchild's wedding is easy. Pick your hard.

I have clients with six children who are making this work. I have clients with brain tumors who are making this work. Everyone's life will present them will challenges, but losing weight is something everyone can do.

Is it hard? Yes.

Can you do it? Absolutely!

15 Making it Stick: How to Maintain Your Weight Loss

YOU WORKED YOUR BUTT OFF to get down to your goal weight. So now what do you do? Let's face it—anybody can lose weight. You can lose weight. But can you keep it off for the rest of your life? That's the key question.

A terrifying statistic says 50% of people who lose weight gain it back again. That's usually because they used a quick fix or a gimmick or a crap-ton of exercise to lose it in the first place. It's not sustainable. I want to encourage you—maintaining your goal weight is not difficult. We haven't come all this way to have you gain it all back in a year. Even if you've done exactly that in the past—especially if you've done that in the past.

All you have to do is follow three rules for maintaining your weight loss. You can get away with straying from the path now and then when you're maintaining. I tend to follow the program 90% of the time, and 10% of the time, I eat something special. (Most of the time, though, I find that treat either doesn't taste as good as I remember, or I get a tummy ache and regret it.)

Here are the three rules for maintaining your weight loss:

1. Step on the scale every day.

2. Keep drinking your water.

3. Keep junk food out of your house.

1. Stay on That Scale

You have to keep weighing yourself. Not because the scale is the end-all and be-all. Not because that's the only way to measure good health—it's not. But that scale is your first line of defense. Get on that scale every single morning, because if it says you're 2 pounds up, that's going to be your first indication that you are off track. What's 2 pounds?

Well, that 2 pounds turns into 4, and that 4 turns into 6, and that 6 will turn into 10. Pretty soon, you're back to being 30, 40, or 50 pounds overweight, because you refused to admit it. That scale is going to keep your desired weight right in the forefront of your mind so you can get back on track before that 2 pounds becomes 10 or 20 and you're back to square one.

Get on that scale, every single morning.

2. Keep Drinking Your Water

Whatever amount of water you drank to get your weight down, you must keep drinking that amount. There are so many positive correlations between water consumption and good health. It's imperative. When you're dehydrated, your body sends signals that it's hungry. Truth is, your body's not really hungry, it's thirsty. If you keep up your water amount, you'll feel full. You'll feel satiated. You'll have energy, you'll stay focused, and you'll even sleep better. So many good things happen when you drink water. Keep drinking!

3. Make Your House a Safe Zone

Never, and I mean never, allow junk food back into your house. There are times when junk food will sneak in, perhaps for a party, or a guest will bring it with them. You've got to get rid of it in less than 24 hours. The longer junk food stays in your house, the greater the chance that you will eat it. And you don't need to do that. Willpower eventually runs out, and that absolutely cannot happen. You can never allow junk food in your house.

That's it. Three simple strategies to follow. If you're happy with your weight now—awesome! If you're not, incorporate these rules now and it will be easier to keep up with them later. They are tried and true, and will maintain your weight loss.

You are amazing.

You deserve to live a long and healthy life.

Backsliding is not going to happen—not this time.

These rules are there to help keep you accountable to yourself and your goal. If you know how much you weigh every day, you will be less likely to swing by Dunkin' Donuts for a croissant. If you are drinking a gallon of water every day, you'll feel too full to crave a snack you know you don't need. And when you get home and still want a snack, you'll have healthier options if you've kept the junk out of your house.

The fact is, maintaining weight loss is so much easier than losing the weight. When you are working toward your goal weight, you're logging everything you eat. You are measuring every teaspoon, every ounce. Once your weight is where you want it to be, it's much easier to maintain, especially if you follow those three rules. They are tried and true, and they work.

How to Add Foods Back In

You've made it! After months of following the process and being extremely good to your body, you have finally reached your goal weight. You're excited, and you want to go out and celebrate.

What do you do? How do you add those forbidden foods back into your daily routine?

The first thing people think of is that list of foods they couldn't eat while they were losing the weight. I can't stress enough that you should *not* reward yourself with food. When you've reached your goal weight, take a trip across the country to see your best friend from college, or buy yourself that cute dress you have been eyeing for months. You should reward yourself, because you have worked awfully hard to get where you are now. But don't do it with food.

That being said, you might be asking yourself, "Well, Cristy, what about those foods you said we could eat again after we reached our goal weight?" Let's talk about those foods.

The first food I like to see my clients add back into their diets is fruit. I am a big believer in fruit. I believe everyone should be eating fruit. The only reason I caution people to avoid it during their weight loss is because it has enough fructose in it to slow people down. However, for people maintaining their goal weight, fruit is perfect. It is loaded with fiber and other important nutrients which make it one of the best snacks you can enjoy.

Yes, an apple has 20 grams of sugar in it. Don't be afraid of fruit when you are maintaining your weight, because there's enough fiber and water in that apple that it will not trigger an insulin response. Nobody is going to get fat eating fruit, I promise.

Start Slowly

This is key: You've got to start slow when you're adding food back in. I'm talking one piece of fruit a day. The reason for this is your own comfort. If you make your goal weight and eat two apples, a banana, and a cup of brown rice in one day, you don't know how your body is going to react to those foods being reintroduced. You could bloat, your stomach might cramp, or your joints could ache.

I know that I cannot metabolize beans. Beans are a great maintenance food, with plenty of protein and fiber, but I simply can't eat them. You may find foods that your body just doesn't want to work with, and you will have an easier time identifying those foods if you pick one from the list per day to try.

So start with one apple or one banana. That way, if your body does react poorly, you will know what caused it.

This goes for any of the wholesome, nutritious foods you held off eating while you were losing your weight. Fruit, lentils (which are also loaded with fiber, by the way), yams, or sweet potatoes. You start with one a day, maintaining your fats, proteins, and veggies the rest of the time.

Be Strategic

You have made it to your goal weight and you feel unstoppable. You know how to feed your body the right food to keep it happy and healthy. At this point, some of my clients want to start adding the occasional carb back in. Say you want an English muffin for breakfast. As with the legumes and fruit, you need to be careful about how you add carbs back in. I have conversations with my clients like this all the time.

They'll tell me they want an English muffin or a bagel and I will ask them what their activity looks like for that day. If they're going to eat that muffin or bagel for breakfast and then go for a run or go to CrossFit, then I tell them to go for it. If their day involves sitting at their computer, then I typically encourage them to hold off on the processed carbs.

I call it planning your carbs. If you know you want that muffin or toast or what-ever it is, schedule it for a time when you will be able to burn it off. I can easily metabolize bread, but I make sure I have it when I have the chance to burn it off that day. Plan your carbs, and earn your starch.

Cheat Meals

So I have talked about the 90/10 method: You eat clean 90% of the time and you can stray for the occasional 10%. A 90/10 week looks like this.

You have to plan ahead for your cheat meal. Like the carbs, you plan your cheat. You want to be doubly sure you have been eating clean right up to that cheat meal.

Say you are meeting a friend on Saturday night and that is going to be your cheat meal. The way you can enjoy that meal is to follow the Code Red process exactly all week long. You get no less than a gallon of water a day, you're eating lots of fat, veggies, and protein all week, and you are getting the sleep you need every night. You do that Sunday through Saturday afternoon, and then Saturday night, you can have your cheat meal.

The next morning, you are right back to drinking your water and eating clean. If you follow this process, the occasional cheat meal is okay. If you are eating clean the rest of the time, you will be fine. One meal is not enough to derail 6 ½ days of clean nutrition.

One thing to be aware of, however, is you may not enjoy that cheat food when you do get it. Miles and I plan one cheat meal a month, and more often than not, I skip it. I seldom feel good after going back to processed food.

So if you are eating clean 90% of the time, you can cheat 10%, but know that it might not agree with you.

Draw Your Line in the Sand

This is it. This next paragraph is how you're going to stay at a healthy weight for the rest of your life! Are you ready?

Pick a number that's about 5–7 pounds above your goal weight. That's your line in the sand. That is **THE NUMBER YOU WILL NOT CROSS**. Got it?

Okay, now when you weigh yourself every day, the second your weight goes above that, you hop right back into weight-loss mode until you lose back down to your goal. Chances are, you've caught it soon enough that it will only take a week or so to get that number back down.

Simple, huh?

This strategy has helped my clients keep their weight off for *years*. And they don't even have to think about it anymore. They can go on vacation and indulge. Then when they get home, they hop back to the weight-loss rules, and any excess weight is gone in no time.

No stress. No blame. No guilt. No fear.

You're such a Rebel!

DIVE IN

16 Food Is Fuel, Nothing Else

IMAGINE YOURSELF IN A BAKERY. You're walking the length of the glass case and peering down on all the sugary treats for sale. As you walk the case you're thinking to yourself, with each item, "I'm turning down that one, that one, those ones, that too..." As you walk to the end, you have turned down every treat. At the very end, you think, "Wow, I did such a good job turning down all those treats. I should reward myself with this croissant here at the end." Counterintuitive, right?

Here's what is happening. Marketing is all about controlling what potential buyers see and when they see it. Marketing in a bakery is putting the best, most appealing items at the end, when people's resolve is at its weakest. People will walk by everything in the case until they see that perfect cupcake or whatever in the last section.

This is a great metaphor for the struggle we all face every day. We face our hardest temptations at night, right? That's because you've made good, strong, willful choices all day. By the time you get home, your willpower is stretched pretty thin. You have worked hard all day, put the kids to bed, and you're relaxing in front of the TV. You were so good all day, so you think it's time for a reward.

Hear this! Nothing could be more detrimental to your success than rewarding or punishing yourself with food.

It is hard though, I know. We were all conditioned as children to view food as a reward. "When you finish your homework, you can have a snack." Or "You got a D in math? Well, no dessert for you for a month, young man!" It's so important for you parents out there not to raise your kids that way. Don't set them up for the struggle you are fighting now. You brought them into this world, and they didn't ask for an unhealthy relationship with food. Don't throw them down the hole you're trying to drag yourself out of. Withholding food from a child is just plain wrong, but using it as a reward is no better.

Unfortunately, our society has always used food as a reward. We celebrate with food in our society. That mentality is a big reason we have the hang-ups with food that we do. The inappropriate emotional relationships we have with food all come from using it as a reward, or making it the focal point of a celebration.

Let's talk about comfort food. Macaroni and cheese. It's chemicals folks, and nothing more. I know it's emotionally tied to Grandma, but macaroni and cheese is just a shot of sugar to your system. Is that comfort? It's a high. It's a direct deposit to the bank of belly fat. You don't need it. Besides, your Grandma would probably rather know you were feeling healthy and happy rather than chowing down on food that's bad for your body.

So food isn't comfort. Food isn't a reward, and it's not a punishment either.

Guys, food is fuel. That's all it is.

It takes a lot of hard work and brain retraining to make this stick, but food is just fuel. You put it into your body to help it work at peak efficiency. It is detrimental to put things in your stomach that don't belong there. You only have about 2 ounces of space in your stomach. Picture a shot glass. That is how much space you have; that is all you need to fill.

So if you only have 2 ounces of space, and your body needs the fuel in that space, you should put the best possible fuel in there, right? Anyone who has raised children knows how little space there is in an infant's bottle. But what goes into that bottle has to be optimal, doesn't it? It has to be clean for that little baby to grow and be healthy.

Therefore, one of your tasks is to remind yourself, as often as you need to for it to sink in, that food is fuel. You need it. You don't withhold gas from your car and expect it to keep running. You need wholesome, nutritious food to be at your very best. If you have a bad day, if you make a mistake at work, or whatever the case may be, you still feed yourself a good, wholesome meal. At the same time, you only give your body what it needs. If you're doing really well, reward yourself with a new blouse or a movie ticket, not food. Cramming a bunch of junk into that 2-ounce space is only going to hurt you.

I'll have clients who don't log any food, and when I ask them why, they'll tell me they didn't lose any weight that day, so they're skipping a meal. That is not okay. You can't operate at your best if you're not giving your body what it needs. That is punishing yourself with food, and not only is it wrong, it doesn't work. You can't just stop feeding yourself.

No matter how big you are, no matter how old you are, it is never too late to change your relationship with food. It's certainly not too late for your kids, if you have them. You are in charge of you, and you have a responsibility to feed yourself wholesome, real food every single day. It is the fuel your body needs.

I am not saying you can't enjoy your food. My husband and I have been to Italy twice, and let me tell you, the food there is just incredible. But think about it, if you're only getting 2 meals a day, you must make them count! That doesn't mean make them big, but make them good.

Reward yourself with something else. You deserve to eat well every day.

Keep It Simple!

As I said earlier, if you can keep your meals to just a few ingredients, you're going to have better results. The more complicated a recipe is, the easier it is to lose track of how much you're actually consuming.

Most typical diet books will give you a huge list of approved recipes and meal plans. I'm not going to do much of that. This section will give you some ideas, but remember— **YOU'RE THE BOSS**. You are taking your life back, which means you are in control. You get to eat what you like. If you hate yogurt, don't eat it! This isn't a diet.

Some people need lots of variety. Some people can eat the same meal over and over again. Either way is fine. It's up to you.

Some people are recipe followers. Some people wing it.

Some are happy just to eat tuna out of a can.

Whichever kind of person you are, that's perfect! Realize that you can change back and forth, too. Maybe you eat tuna out of a can 6 days a week, and then decide to create an amazing gourmet meal on Saturday night. It's your life— take it back.

Meal Plan and Prep

It doesn't matter whether you're a parent, grandparent, or single executive on the go, we all have busy lives. One of the best things you can do to ensure your success is to plan your meals in advance. Decisions take energy. And meal planning takes one more decision off your plate for the rest of the week. At the very least, take 10 minutes and jot down what you think you'd like to eat for dinner all week. You can always change your mind later. But this gives you

a starting point. If you want to, you can add breakfast and lunch to your plan. Many of my clients simply have cream in their coffee and are good until lunchtime when they just have something simple packed for work.

At the other end of the spectrum is food prepping. Some people love spending a Sunday afternoon doing all the shopping and prep work (especially chopping veggies) for the week. If that's you, great! You can get most of your lunches bagged and your dinners ready for the oven within a short, condensed time. Other people, though, find that if they prep all the food for the week, it just gets eaten faster. So go with what makes you happy and makes your busy week easier.

Get a Few Good Appliances

I don't cook. My husband, Miles, does that for our household. But Code Red Rebels from all over swear by a few key appliances like the Instapot and an air fryer. Ninja and immersion blenders can come in handy, too. Some of my clients find that as they get rid of their toasters and panini presses, they can reward themselves with new appliances that help them keep to the Code Red Lifestyle.

Prepare Fallback Meals

Even the best-laid meal plans can get tossed aside by a late meeting or soccer game. It's great to have approved meals that are already prepared, so you can grab them instead of fast food or a frozen pizza. Freezing your leftovers can even do in a pinch.

How to Replace Bread for Sandwiches, Burgers, and Pizza

Bread isn't as tough to give up when you know how to make your favorite foods without it. So here are some ideas to help you out.

HOT SANDWICHES: Just heat up the ingredients and make a "skillet." This is especially yummy for reubens.

COLD SANDWICHES AND BURGERS: Make a lettuce wrap instead. Use a large, soft-leaf lettuce like Boston Bibb or the top half of a romaine leaf for the bread replacement. You can do a top and bottom leaf, or make a rollup. I love making BLTs (bacon, lettuce, and tomato sandwiches) this way. Many restaurants will happily give you a lettuce-wrapped burger. You won't even miss the bun.

You can also make an "inside-out" sandwich by using the meat as the outer layer, adding some mayo or guacamole and veggies, then rolling it up!

PIZZA: This is a tough one, but recipe creators have been working tirelessly to perfect the grain-free pizza crust. These are usually made from grated cauliflower and cheese, so you might want to wait until maintenance mode to try this. But you can also make mini "pizza cups" to satisfy that pepperoni craving. Put large pepperoni slices into a greased muffin tin. Add a teaspoon of sugar-free marinara and maybe an olive or grated mushroom. Bake them in the oven for a few minutes—yum!

CLOUD BREAD: Remember that I don't cook, okay? This recipe is a favorite in the high-fat, low-carb community. But it can be tricky to get just right. It's basically a bread substitute using eggs and cream of tartar (not tartar sauce!). You can find lots of recipes for cloud bread online.

SUNDAYS ARE FOR BRAIN PREP

In health and fitness circles, Sundays have always been meal-prep days. Check it out on Instagram or Pinterest—tons of pictures of bodybuilders and fitness people lining up all their Tupperware and 50 chicken breasts. You can see me doing it on my Instagram, too.

If you think about it, Sundays make sense because most people have that day off. People use it to cook up their bacon, broccoli, chicken, or whatever they are eating consistently, so they're organized for the week. It's a great way to get yourself ahead of your food.

But what about brain prep?

What do you do to get your mind ready for the upcoming week? You might think it's silly, but sticking to a food plan and making healthy decisions all day can be mentally exhausting. What you tell yourself leading up to a new week will impact how that week goes. Think about how you get yourself into the right mindset on Sunday.

You could fall apart. Some people dread Mondays enough that Sunday is a bummer, too. "I don't want Sunday to end, I don't want to go back to work," they moan. Or if you're a parent, maybe your kids have soccer matches out of town, or late practices that you're dreading. Maybe you are in a difficult relationship, or dealing with an aging parent. I don't know what you're facing, but think about where your head is on Sunday.

I call it borrowing trouble. You're worrying yourself sick over things that haven't even happened yet. Don't borrow trouble. Just take one thing at a time when it happens. What I suggest is spend some time on Sunday planning out how you want your week to go. I'm not saying sit on a mat and meditate, I am saying envision the upcoming week on your terms.

Remember, your words have power. Tell yourself that your week is going to go well. Stand in front of your mirror and tell yourself that your weight is still going down, that your body is healing a bit more every day. Focus your attention on gratitude for everything you have, and everything that is going well. Tell yourself that you're beautiful, and that you're excellent at what you do. Use Sunday as a day to front-load positivity into your week. Talk yourself up, and visualize yourself where you want to be.

I plan way ahead. I tell myself what I'm going to say on the morning show on a promotion tour that hasn't happened yet. I visualize myself walking out, all lean and ripped, and telling my story. I see myself telling the world about a poor farm girl with nothing who made it out of an abusive relationship to achieve great success.

It's okay to think ahead, but do it on your terms. Don't borrow trouble; put yourself in the future accomplishing what you want. Maybe that's deadlifting 295 pounds. Maybe it's running a mile, or being able to wear a bikini next summer. Whatever your goals are, focus on them and visualize yourself achieving them.

You are taking your life back, and people see what you do. It's spreading to your family, your friends, and coworkers. Think about how your success will influence countless other people to improve their lives, and the lives of their children. It is okay to want good things, and to want big things for yourself.

Start your brain prep for the week on Sunday and live it out the rest of the week. Plan for your success.

How to Replace Pasta and Rice

What is pasta, really? It doesn't taste like anything on its own. For most of us, it's just a vehicle for all that yummy sauce. There are some really great pasta alternatives that let you enjoy your pesto or marinara sauce as much or more than you used to.

ZUCCHINI NOODLES (OR ZOODLES): Make long, spaghetti-like strands using a spiralizer or julienne vegetable peeler. These can be cooked or

eaten raw. They make a great cold pasta salad!

SPAGHETTI SQUASH: The inside of this squash looks just like spaghetti. (Clever name, huh?) Once it's baked, you just use a fork to separate the strands. Be careful to let it cool a bit first. Those suckers are hot!

CAULIFLOWER RICE: If you're making a stir-fry or craving Chinese food, grated cauliflower makes a great substitute. It's a versatile veg that easily takes on the flavors of the sauces or spices it's cooked with. You can use a food processor or just a regular old cheese grater to get the right consistency. Watch your fingers!

MEAT: What? Use meat as a substitute for pasta? Well, why not? Try adding that basil pesto to a nice piece of salmon or shrimp. Make a bun-less sloppy joe with just ground beef and marinara sauce. You might discover you never needed pasta in the first place.

Breakfast Ideas

Please don't get hung up on breakfast food. Be a Rebel! If you want to eat leftover steak or a big tuna salad for your first meal of the day, awesome. And if you are happy with just coffee until noon, great. Don't eat if you're not hungry. People always ask me for breakfast ideas, though. So here goes.

- Avocados
- Bacon
- Berries (raw or in a smoothie)
- Cloud bread
- Eggs
- Greek yogurt (full-fat)
- Mini-quiche
- Omelet
- Sausage

Lunch Ideas

Lunch can be your main meal for the day, or it can just be something quick to tide you over until dinnertime. Remember you'll probably be eating that last meal much earlier than you're used to.

- Almond butter on celery

- Berries
  (fresh or frozen, smoothie)

- Bun-less burger

- Inside-out sandwiches
  (meat rollups)

- Jerky

- Lettuce wraps

- Oven-roasted veggies

- Salad with or without meat

- Meat or fish (any you like)

- Veggies dipped in sour cream
  or Greek yogurt

Dinner Ideas

You are eating before 6:30, right? Keep it simple. Just pick a meat and a vegetable, and maybe some berries or a square of extra dark chocolate for a little treat. Don't make dinner into a big production, unless you really enjoy cooking. Beware of pre-packaged meats like meatballs, sausages, and crabmeat. Sometimes companies add grain-based fillers to make the food cheaper to produce.

ANY MEAT: beef, chicken, crab, fish, lobster, pork, shrimp,

ANY VEGETABLE (EXCEPT STARCHY VEG LIKE POTATOES AND SWEET POTATOES)**:** raw, roasted, or steamed; keep sauces and dressings to a minimum

FAJITA ROLLUPS: flat steaks with peppers and onions rolled up inside

"SPAGHETTI": Use one of the pasta substitutes with a sugar-free meat and marinara sauce.

PULLED PORK: Who doesn't love pork barbecue? It takes a good 12–16 hours to slow-cook pulled pork properly. So plan ahead! And skip the ketchup-based sauce and go for the Eastern Carolina sauce; it's just vinegar and red pepper.

MEATLOAF AND MASHED "POTATOES": Swap out those bread crumbs for pork rinds and you're good. Go easy on the ketchup. And mash up some lightly steamed cauliflower instead of potatoes. Tasty!

CHICKEN SALAD: Just mix up some chopped chicken breast with mayo and celery. Add salt and pepper and serve. So fast and easy.

SALAD: Add some chicken or steak to your favorite salad vegetables. Presto!

LETTUCE TACOS: Include everything but the shell. Brown some ground beef with spices. Spoon it into lettuce leaves with a little salsa and sour cream.

Snack Ideas

Water! Seriously, you don't need to snack. A big bottle of water can help you get over your urge to munch on something. Add some Mio flavoring or lemon slices. Okay, but sometimes you just want a little something. Here are some ideas. Just don't forget to weigh, measure, and log it in.

- Avocado

- Berries

- Celery sticks or cucumber slices with a *little* bit of sour cream or cream cheese

- Extra dark chocolate (unless this causes cravings for more sugar)

- Jerky

- Nuts

Sara Hafliger

This 38-Year-Old Mom Lost 67 Pounds and Can Now Keep Up With Her 4 Children

MY STORY begins around the time I became a mother. I had never been overweight, but I was always one of those people who gained weight easily. Knowing that, I was always pretty good about keeping myself where I felt comfortable.

My trouble started a few years ago. My husband and I decided we wanted children, and I had a miscarriage, which is a terrible experience. I was depressed and I was scared. I decided to see some fertility

doctors to try and figure out why I was having trouble getting pregnant.

I wasn't getting anywhere or hearing any good news. I began to get more depressed, and started to experience anxiety as well. Finally, I was told I might never get pregnant. As a woman, to hear a doctor tell you that is one of the worst things you could ever imagine hearing. I didn't know what was wrong with me, and this was when I started really struggling with emotional eating.

Then out of the blue, I managed to get pregnant. I was overjoyed! During that first pregnancy, however, I gained 50 pounds. The doctors assured me that with breastfeeding, that weight would go away, but it didn't. Then I got pregnant again, and gained more weight on top of the 50 pounds I had packed on with my first child.

My husband and I were blessed with two more children after that, and with each child, I gained more and more weight, never making it back to my original weight. At that point, I was 250 pounds and utterly miserable. Here I was with four beautiful children but I had no energy to go out and have fun with them.

I was too depressed, too embarrassed of my body to go out in public. I mean, I

didn't even want to go grocery shopping or be seen by anyone, because of how I looked. I made excuses not to see friends, just to avoid people seeing me. It gets awfully hot in Idaho, and I didn't even want to take my kids to the pool because there was no way I wanted to get into a bathing suit.

I can't even remember how many diets I tried. Nutrisystem, Medifast, Plexus, you name it. Looking back, I hate to think how much I spent on diets that didn't work.

Ultimately, a friend of mine, Tara, inspired me when I saw pictures of her on Facebook. It caught my attention because, like me, she never used to post pictures of herself because of her weight. She would only ever post pictures of her kids. So then I see this new picture of her and my mouth literally dropped open. She looked amazing! I emailed her right away and asked if she wouldn't mind telling me how she did it.

That was how I first heard about Cristy, and suddenly, everything just clicked. I signed up for her 90-day program. It was an immediate decision for me. I decided then and there that I would not cheat. I told myself that I had already spent a lot of money, and I didn't want to fail again.

Don't get me wrong, I was nervous. I knew that if I was hungry, I wasn't going to make it. I had failed so many other diets because I would get hungry and then break down and eat. But I knew I had to try, or I would be fat forever.

March 17th of 2017 was my first day on the program. My family was leaving for vacation in California on March 19th, so I thought for sure Cristy would let me start when I got back. I emailed to let her know we would be leaving in two days and she got right back to me saying, "Have fun! I expect you to stick to the program while you're away." Honestly, Cristy scares me a little bit, but that is exactly what I needed.

I needed someone tough to make me stick with it and hold me accountable to my commitment to myself.

With her support, I made it through my vacation without one slipup. I packed breakfasts and lunches for the entire trip, and I was faithful to the plan the *entire* time. I was fortunate too, because most people who have done this will tell you that the first week is awful. When people are detoxing from sugar, it takes about a week of feeling terrible before you start to feel really good.

I think it was because I was on the road, but I was fine. Either I didn't notice the symptoms because of travel, or it just wasn't as difficult for me. I don't know, but I felt pretty good the whole time. The biggest adjustment for me was quitting Diet Coke. I used to drink Diet Coke all the time, even first thing in the morning. I haven't had one since I started, and I don't miss it. So between March and June of 2017, I have lost 64 pounds, and I know I'm not done. Already though, I feel so much better.

There have been so many positive changes in my life just over the last few months—I feel amazing. I used to have terrible acid reflux, to the point where I couldn't lie flat at night. I had to take

Protonix daily, but now it's completely gone. I have the energy to play with my kids. I mean, even something as simple as bending over to tie a shoe is easier now. My depression and anxiety are gone, and we even have a family picture scheduled for July. I am just so excited!

offer; anyone who is willing to put in the work will be successful with her.

So if you're just starting this lifestyle, stick with it, drink your water, and trust Cristy 100%. She knows what she is doing and you *will* be successful if you follow the

Don't get me wrong, I was nervous. I knew that if I was hungry, I wasn't going to make it. I had failed so many other diets because I would get hungry and then break down and eat. But I knew I had to try, or I would be fat forever.

I've been to the pool about 10 times with my kids, and I am not embarrassed anymore. I love going out in public now. People stop me and ask what I'm doing and compliment me. I *never* used to talk about my diets, but now I am telling everyone I can about Cristy. She has so much to

rules. If you're not quite sure about trying the Code Red Lifestyle—do it! I was so unhealthy, and looking back now, Cristy really saved my life.

Do it now. You won't regret it!

17 What to Do When Your Family is Not on Board

LET'S TALK ABOUT YOUR FAMILY. Long-term relationships, significant others—whatever you call the person you live and share your space with. Very rarely are couples 100% on the same page with each other. There's a big difference between your spouse saying, "You know, I'd like to lose some weight" and your spouse committing to the Code Red Lifestyle. Your spouse might say they're on board, but they might not be committed to the program the way that you are.

Let's face it—it's easy to agree to a diet after a big dinner. Once you're full, a diet sounds like a great idea. Unfortunately, as soon as your spouse gets a sugar craving, they're done. So with the best of intentions, your spouse will try to be on board with you, but unless they are committed to the same program you are, they will struggle to do what you are doing.

The commitment is a serious one. I ask people to clear out their cupboards when they commit, because a sugar craving will prevent weight loss. Remember that a sugar craving is a chemical addiction 8 times stronger than a cocaine addiction. Say you only keep a box of Lucky Charms in the pantry for the kids. When you're dieting and that sugar craving hits, that box of cereal won't just be for the kids anymore. In the early part of your program, refusing a sugar craving is hard, and if you have any sugar in the house, you will most likely eat it. One of the golden rules is keep junk food out of your house. If it's not in your house, you're much less likely to give in to those cravings.

So when your spouse says they want to lose weight and they're on board with you, that means they need to help you clean out the pantry. That means they need to stop bringing junk food home too. About 75% of my clients tell me their spouses help them clean out the cupboard, but there's usually about 25% who say that their significant others aren't as cooperative. That is a conflict, and one that will make your weight-loss journey harder.

Okay, so you need all the sugar out of the house, but your spouse demands their nightly bowl of ice cream or chips. What do you do?

First off, for this to work, you have to be 100% committed. If you're not ready to change your life, then nobody anywhere will be able to make you do it. There were times in your past when you weren't ready to make a change, right? If someone had come along back then and told you to change, you would have told them to get lost. So if your spouse isn't ready to give up their stupid chips, don't fight them over it. Don't bully them into changing, because it's not going to work.

I recommend trying to make a compromise. If your spouse isn't ready to give up their junk food, get them to hide it. Tell them to keep it in their shop or in their man-cave or in their office. I had a client who asked her husband to keep his junk food in his truck, and he agreed to that. If your spouse isn't ready to change, then you can't force it, but they should be able to make a concession that helps you out on your journey.

For example, my husband is a gourmet chef. He makes phenomenal, mouth-watering dinners. They're all meat and veggies, but they're rich and delicious.

I do not eat dinner. I found that eating at night made it too hard for me to keep my weight where I wanted it. I asked my husband if he could make a big lunch instead of dinner, and he flat out refused. I clean up after dinner, so even if my willpower kept me from eating at the table, 9 times out of 10 I ate off the pan while I was cleaning up. And, folks, it doesn't matter if you eat at the table or in the kitchen.

We had a big fight about the dinners, but the compromise we made was that I would not attend dinner. Whether I go to another room to paint or take the dog for a walk, I am not present for dinner. So now my husband either cooks less or makes some for me to have for lunch the following day. I still do the dishes, but he has agreed to put all the food away so I'm not tempted to sneak while I'm cleaning up. This is one example of a compromise you can make with your spouse if they are not dieting the same way you are.

Another good strategy is use "we" instead of "you." Let's say your spouse is cooking spaghetti and marinara for himself and the kids. Instead of telling him, "You know that's all just sugar, right?" try rephrasing it like "What are we adding for protein?" Because look, if you guys are married, or deeply committed to each other, it should be "we."

Lead by example. Don't push or nag your spouse, because they'll only dig in their heels. People can be awfully stubborn, and trying to goad them one way or another will only make them resist that change more. Instead, just let them see the positive changes in yourself. You stick to what you're doing and let the results do the talking. Because your spouse loves you. They love every inch of you, and they will notice when you start shrinking. They will hear the compliments you get from your friends and family. Let them just watch you transform your life.

I encourage you to avoid reporting every pound lost as well. Especially if your spouse is also trying to lose weight. If you tell them about every pound, they might take that as you rubbing it in. It's hard, because you're so proud of each pound you lose, and you should be. But when it comes to reporting it to your spouse, maybe just stick to the milestones—10, 15, 20 pounds—however you want to mark your success.

Now, I used to advise people, when they committed to weight loss, to go in and wipe out their cupboards. However, if you have a spouse or a family, going in and annihilating your pantry is just asking for a fight. Instead, espe-cially if you have children, slowly stop replacing the junk food. Ease your family into healthier options in the cupboard. Once the Oreos are gone, replace them with fruit. If you don't drastically remove all the junk food, your family will be less likely to notice the changes.

To sum this up, you don't have to cause World War III with your family if they're not on board with your weight-loss program. You can still be perfectly suc-cessful with your own goals even if they're still eating their daily bowl of Raisin Bran. (By the way, Raisin Bran is the worst possible cereal. Highest sugar and carb mix you could ever ask for.) But all you need to do is stick to the program for yourself, and your body will do all the talking. Don't hound your spouse. Let them watch you drop the pounds. And they will watch, believe me. Eventually they will come around, but not if you nag them.

Carole Seigler Terherst

This 64-Year-Old Grandmother Lost 20 Pounds and ALL Her Pain

(Even Cristy's mom has to follow the rules.)

I'VE NEVER been really overweight, and there have been times when I've been really skinny. But I remember right after we had grandkids, I noticed I was feeling a bit squishy around the middle. And I remember thinking to myself, "That's okay, I'm going to be one of those soft, huggable grandmas." What I was really doing was convincing myself that I wanted to be soft and squishy. My grandmothers were like that, and I figured that's how it would be for me. I just thought getting larger was what happened when you got to be in your 50s and had grandkids.

BUT I DON'T WANT TO "GET OLD"

Even though I was trying to accept this whole "squishy grandma" thing, deep down I really didn't want to. The extra weight just bugged me. About that time, Cristy came home to visit us. This was when she was a personal trainer in New York, and hadn't really honed in on the Code Red nutritional lifestyle. So she had me running up mountains and doing all this exercise to get the weight off.

Now, I don't mind being active. I'll go for a walk or ride a horse, but I don't really like to "exercise." And all this work wasn't exactly melting the pounds off. So

I started thinking about creative ways to hide those few extra pounds, like changing my hairstyle or my clothes.

loss. I started watching her videos and we talked on the phone. And I began to really look at what I was cooking and eating.

Don't for one second believe that lie that you're "too old" to lose weight and turn your life around. Whatever age you are, it doesn't matter. You can absolutely get healthier and feel better when you eat the right foods, drink water, and get enough sleep.

Some time later, Cristy really figured out the nutrition component and started helping people experience some amazing weight

I figured I could do anything for 30 days, so I had her write up a nutrition plan for me. Back then, I was in pain *all the time*, especially in my fingers and wrists. I just figured I was getting older and this must be arthritis. That happens when you get older, right? I wasn't on any medication or anything, but the pain was there every night. It didn't really go away until I went to sleep.

So I followed the plan she made for me. I didn't cheat at all. The first week was tough, getting off sugar, but other than that it was pretty simple. I lost the weight I wanted to and felt great. But I was so busy that I just went about my life as normal. Then about a month into it, I stopped dead in my tracks one day. And I looked at my hands. And I realized the pain was *gone*. It wasn't just a little bit better—it was 100% gone!

I told Cristy about it and she said, "Mom, I think it's the grains. You've gotten rid of the inflammation." That made sense, and I didn't really think any more about it. Until I got a craving for some Chinese food. I went out and picked up some takeout chicken with rice. Oh, the next morning! I was puffy, my knuckles hurt—it was terrible. And that's when I got it. Everything my daughter had said about the grains was right.

At that point, I had two choices. I could moan and groan, suffer through the pain, take my pain relievers, and just chalk it up to old age. Or I could knock that crap off and stop eating the foods that made me hurt! Instead I could choose to eat the food that made me wake up with a burst of energy so I could do the housework, get the meals cooked, and be out the door to work by 8 a.m. After I realized that, I really had no choice but to follow the Code Red rules.

I was excited about the 20-pound weight loss, but I was so much more excited to be pain-free. These days, whenever I eat

pasta or accidentally have some grains in a sauce or something, I pay for it the next morning. The pain comes back every time.

I know my numbers. I know the rules. And sometimes I still let my weight creep up or I get behind on my water. But once it gets to a certain point, I have to just say, "No more." And that's when I have to get serious about following the rules for weight-loss mode until I get back to where I want to be.

STAYING ACTIVE IS THE BEST REWARD

My husband, Larry, was able to stop taking so many medications. He loves to go hunting and be outdoors. He can run around with the grandkids and then go chop a tree down. We aren't just "being" grandparents. We are "doing" the grandparent thing. We're active. We're running around and swimming and playing games outside. We are actively participating in their lives. And that's how it should be.

Here's how I see it. If you do nothing, in a month or a year you'll be exactly where you are now or worse. If you take action, follow the rules, and make friends with the other Code Red Rebels, you're going to feel better. I want to be as healthy as I can for as long as I can. And I've seen so many people take their lives back with Cristy's program, I know anyone can do this. Age is not an excuse.

18 Healthy Desserts and Snacks for Your Family

YOU KNOW HOW HARD IT IS to try to eat all the right things while watching your kids eat all the wrong things? You're not alone. America has a serious childhood obesity epidemic, and sugar is one of the main reasons. Sugar is the cocaine of the food world, and it's causing our country some major health problems.

Sugar. It all comes down to sugar.

The average American child consumes 150 grams of sugar every day, and that is the low end. Some of the kids I've seen are getting 300–400 grams a day. That's bullcrap! Kids don't need that.

Just because they can metabolize it doesn't mean they need it. Kids these days have the sweetest palates. Milk isn't good enough anymore, now they need chocolate milk. It would be great if your kids just ate their veggies and didn't complain, but we all know that isn't going to happen. Think about your own struggle with sugar. Think about how hard you're working right now to change your relationship with food. Think about how hard America's kids are going to have to work when they're your age.

I am not a mother, and sometimes my opinions about children don't really fly because I haven't raised my own. I feel like every mom should be able to say, "I'm the parent, you can't have Lucky Charms, end of story." But mothers out there have a real fight on their hands with their kids. I am not going to tell you how to do it, but I will offer some healthier alternatives to some of your kids' favorite sweets.

Walden Farms makes a variety of sugar-free products that are all quite good. They offer sugar-free, calorie-free, and fat-free items that still taste good without the added sugar. They make salad dressings, mayonnaise, pancake syrups, jellies, jams, coffee creamers, and more.

Most of the healthy snacks I suggest for your family are based around fruit. As you know, while you are in the process of losing weight, you want to avoid fruit yourself because while it's not going to make you fat, it will slow the weight-loss process. But fruit is a healthy alternative to cookies, cakes, and other sweet snacks.

One treat I occasionally enjoy is apple slices with dark chocolate melted over them. This has to be very dark chocolate, like Lindt's 85% or 90% cocoa variety. The higher the percentage of cocoa, the better. However, if you're not used to it, that high a percentage will taste bitter. You can adjust your taste buds slowly by starting with 60% and working your way up. You can also make your own whipped cream at home with no sugar as a tasty dip for apple slices. Another snack I enjoy is coconut and dark chocolate dip. You melt the chocolate in the microwave, add some coconut extract, and have that with apple slices.

While we're at it, let's talk about apples. They are packed with fiber, always an excellent option if you are maintaining your goal weight. Apples and bananas do have sugar, but it's a more natural form of sugar. When you get down to your goal weight and you're maintaining, you can enjoy these healthy desserts too.

You can do so much with apples as far as snacks or desserts go. There are all kinds of sugar-free caramels you can melt and drizzle over sliced apples, and they're delicious. Some kids really like peanut butter. If you choose to buy peanut butter, spend a little more and get 100% natural. Avoid Jif, Skippy, and all the other sugar-laden brands. Skip the Nutella as well. There is nothing healthy about Nutella. It's crammed with sugar.

Here are some other alternatives to sugary foods:

- Bananas with cream

- Berries sprinkled with Splenda or stevia

- Blueberries with cream

- Greek yogurt with berries, sugar-free drizzle, or chia seeds (for texture)

- Strawberries with cream

And for folks who crave salty or savory snacks, you can offer your family some of these:

- Beef jerky

- Celery or carrots with hummus

- Cheese sticks

- Popcorn: not microwaved, not caramel corn, and not kettle corn; plain popcorn with real butter and a little bit of salt (Admit it, you like it better that way anyway.)

As with the fruit, these are not snacks you want to have while you are in weight-loss mode. Hummus is super healthy, but it is calorie-dense, so it's something you want to avoid while you're losing weight. However, these are perfectly healthy options for your family, especially your kids. They can metabolize this stuff with no problem, and they won't be bouncing off the walls right before bed.

Presentation is everything. If you want your family to eat healthy food, make it fun! Instead of telling them they can't have Oreos anymore because they're bad, offer a new snack like it's some huge treat. I'll never forget when I learned this lesson. One year for Christmas, my family was so poor that my parents couldn't buy us any presents. Instead of telling us we were poor, my mother made my sisters and me dolls that matched our eyes and hair color. She made them by hand and presented them to us in a way that was so special. It was the best Christmas ever. We each got a handmade doll and an orange. And because my mother presented them to us in such a special way, we thought it was the best.

Find a way to present healthier food to your kids in a way that they think they're getting a special treat. Put it in a fancy glass dish, or color the whipped cream. Whatever you can do to make it fun. Fruit is readily available these days, it's colorful, and you can really dress it up and have fun with it.

REBEL
FOR LIFE

19

How to Eat Out and Stay on Track

ONE OF THE BEAUTIFUL THINGS about the Code Red Lifestyle is its simplicity. You'll be amazed how much money you can save by making a quick dinner at home rather than going out to a restaurant. And don't get me started on all the crap you won't be buying at the grocery store like soda, snack foods, and sugar-laden condiments.

But what if you like to eat out? Or you travel for business? Or band rehearsal went late and you need to grab something on the way home? You absolutely can eat out and continue to lose weight. You can even eat at fast-food joints and stay on the program. (Gasp!) Obviously, I'd prefer you cook a nice steak at home over grabbing a burger at McDonald's. But sometimes fast food happens. This is about integrating healthy choices into *your* life. You are the boss.

The problem with eating out is you don't really know what you're eating, or how much. So you have to do some detective work. Fortunately, there are menus to consult and people to ask. The key is to go in prepared. Know what you're going to order ahead of time, if at all possible. Pull up the menu on the restaurant website or Facebook. Scan through for calorie counts. Fast-food joints and mid-level chain restaurants almost always have a card with nutrition facts for all their menu items. You just have to ask for it. That card will give you the complete breakdown on all your choices so you can make an informed decision.

I tell my clients to bring a food scale and measuring spoons with them when they eat out. But I get that it's awkward to whip out a scale and weigh your steak during a business meeting. So find out ahead of time or ask the server how many ounces the steak or chicken weighs. And ask about how it's prepared. What oils is it cooked in? Are there any glazes or sauces? Can you get them on the side or just eliminate them? I sometimes call the manager ahead of time to get all this sorted out so I don't have to give the poor server a long list of questions.

Here are some guidelines to help you make better choices when eating out.

AVOID THE ITEMS YOU KNOW YOU CAN'T EAT. Breadsticks? Desserts? French fries? Right out. So don't even order them. If they come with a meal, ask if you can substitute steamed veggies or a salad.

STICK TO MEAT AND VEGGIES. Try to choose something that you might normally eat at home. A grilled chicken breast, seafood, or a nice juicy steak. Steamed, grilled, or raw vegetables are great, as long as you're avoiding potatoes, sweet potatoes, and corn. Stay away from breading and fancy sauces, keep it as plain and simple as possible. If the chicken is dry and bland, ask for some butter and use that to moisten it a bit.

MAKE SPECIAL REQUESTS, ESPECIALLY FOR FAST FOOD. Your kid's favorite fast-food joint isn't going to advertise this, but you can request a burger without the bun or cheese. If you tell them you're on a restricted diet, they will get it. (Even though this isn't a diet, they don't have to know that.)

You can ask for just the eggs and bacon from a breakfast platter. Or just tell them what you are looking for and ask what they recommend. I've been on the road and ordered at the drive-thru window. I just say, "You know the grilled chicken sandwich? Can I just have the chicken?" It was about 5 ounces, came in a nice box, cost about $2, and was just enough for me. Most places will be very accommodating. But you won't know if you don't ask.

SKIP THE COCKTAILS, OR OFFER TO BE THE DESIGNATED DRIVER. If you're used to having wine or a cocktail with dinner, this one can be tough. But alcohol is absolutely on the Foods to Avoid list. Have a tall glass of water or some hot tea, and be proud of yourself. If someone asks why you're not drinking, just smile and say, "I'm a Rebel!"

CONSIDER ORDERING FROM THE APPETIZER MENU. Most restaurant portion sizes are huge—way more than we really need to be satisfied. So think about ordering from the appetizer menu as your main meal. The portions will be smaller, and you'll spend less money too.

ENJOY THE COMPANY, AND DON'T FOCUS ON THE FOOD. So what do you do when you have to wait 30 minutes in line and you know you're not going to make the 6:30 eating window? Or you're just really not that hungry? How about just ordering a glass of water and enjoying the company of your friends and family? I know it sounds strange, but it is possible to sit in a restaurant and not order anything to eat. If it's too awkward, you could always say you ate a late lunch (which could be entirely true).

Remember, food is fuel. Not entertainment.

Michelle Boyd-Keenan & Nichole Curtis

These Sisters Worked Together to Overcome Frustration After Years of Failed Diets and Lost 120 Pounds Between Them

LOSING WEIGHT has been a constant battle for both of us. I gained a lot of weight after having kids and really just not paying attention to my body. We spent money on everything we could think of to lose weight. Michelle went on her first diet in 6th grade, and struggled as her weight went up and down and eventually just stayed up.

We both worked out regularly and couldn't understand why it was so hard to stay healthy. Eventually, we both got to the point where we just accepted that we were heavy and that was how it was going to be forever. But we were definitely depressed. We didn't feel like ourselves. Michelle describes it as being surrounded by fat so the real her couldn't get out.

OUR TURNING POINTS

Michelle had stalked Cristy online for ages and thought we should try her Code Red program. I looked it up online and wondered *Why would this work? What makes this any different from the dozens of other diets we've tried?* Then I went upstairs and got ready for bed. The moment that stopped me in my tracks was when I had to squeeze into my pajama bottoms. And I thought *This is just ridiculous*. I shouldn't have to work hard to pull my large PJs over my rear. So I messaged Michelle and said, "Okay, what's her website again?" That's when I had just had enough. It was time to change.

We had tried and given up on so many different ways to lose weight and nothing worked for very long. But Michelle had

Cristy and it was the **BEST DECISION I EVER MADE**.

I used to eat until my stomach felt like it would burst. We were always taught to clean our plates no matter what. It was hard, but we learned to listen to our bodies and only eat when we were truly

It's weird how people get used to their pain. We get used to our joints hurting. We accept that we can't get to the top of the stairs without panting. We just push it to the back of our minds and go on with life.

friends who had been successful with Cristy. So we decided to trust what we saw with our own eyes and give it a try.

Being at rock bottom feels awful. We were desperate, and really weren't sure what to expect. But meeting Cristy was so exciting. She explained everything so clearly, and for the first time, we really felt like we had hope. So I decided that it was time to take care of me. And I was going to make this work no matter what. I actually took out a loan to get a personal program with

hungry. I actually *sleep* now! I've got energy and I'm happy. I want to go places and do things. The transformation has been amazing. I feel like a different person.

One huge benefit of the Code Red Lifestyle is that we get to eat real food that we can just go buy at the grocery store. There are no pills or shakes we have to spend extra money on and order through the mail. This is just real life. Shopping at any grocery store like a normal person. You don't have to be a millionaire or go to the doctor every week to do it.

THE BIGGEST SURPRISE

The biggest surprise to me was that I wasn't hungry! Every diet I've been on works okay for a little while. But then along comes a holiday or a birthday party and there are all kinds of cakes and cookies and yummy food. Let me tell you, it's so much easier to walk away from that stuff if you're not hungry. Most of the time, I would give in. But not anymore.

You're not starving to death on this program. So it's easy to give up the stuff that's bad for you and makes you feel terrible. People ask me what pills I'm taking to lose weight, and I tell them I'm not taking any. I mean, what are you going to do? Take pills for the rest of your life? No! I'm on bacon and eggs. That's sustainable.

We both started around 185 and we're both down to the 120s. Neither one of us ever thought we'd see 125. We thought we'd be lucky to get to 140. And when we finally got to goal weight, it was such a shock!

The support from the Code Red community makes such a huge difference. Cristy believes *fiercely* that you can do this. And she won't accept anything less than your best. That means the difference between walking past a fudge brownie and stuffing

it into your mouth. These people are part of our family now.

We've both been able to keep living our normal lives while continuing to lose weight. We both traveled and managed to keep losing even on vacation. That never happens on other programs! We took our food scales, measuring spoons, and bathroom scales with us and just did what we had to do. And best of all, we had fun!

The biggest thing is to be prepared. We cook our food and bring it with us. We are

never without our water bottles and little snacks like cashew butter and pepperoni sticks. So no matter where we go, we are always prepared and never hungry.

LISTENING TO OUR BODIES

It's weird how people get used to their pain. We get used to our joints hurting. We accept that we can't get to the top of the stairs without panting. We just push it to the back of our minds and go on with life. But those signs are our bodies' way of **WARNING US THAT WE ARE NOT HEALTHY**. We should be paying

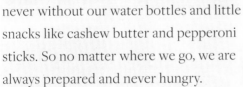

attention to those warning signs and *doing something*.

Within a week or two of starting the Code Red Lifestyle, you really notice the changes. One of the first things we both noticed was how much better we were sleeping. For some reason, when you take all the crap out of your diet, you wake up in the morning feeling refreshed. You feel like you actually got some sleep. No one *ever* told us that sleep affected weight loss. And we had studied and tried so many programs. None of them mentioned sleep.

How can you put a price tag on your happiness and your health? We were both pre-diabetic, but we're not anymore. I had gastric problems that have gone away. We're happy and healthy and have the tools to stay that way forever.

With this book, you have the tools in your hand. Trust the program. Follow the rules. Even if they don't make complete sense to you. Even if they are the opposite of what you've been told. Just trust Cristy. Read the success stories. If you're struggling with your weight and you think you know what you're doing, you will be amazed what happens when you take a chance and try something different.

Take your life back. It doesn't get better than this!

20 The Truth About Alcohol

DURING WEIGHT-LOSS MODE, there's no alcohol allowed. Period. Even if you don't drink those sweetened fruity umbrella drinks, alcohol metabolizes in the liver and turns into sugar. And that's what we're trying to avoid. I've never seen anyone experience consistent weight loss while drinking alcohol.

Another issue with alcohol is that it makes you lose your inhibitions. And while you might not be worried about dancing on tabletops or drunk-texting your ex, you could seriously damage your weight-loss efforts. You're not going to care about your commitment to yourself, and you're much more likely to throw caution to the wind and eat whatever snack foods are put in front of you. Think about it. What else do you do when you're drinking? You eat! Peanuts. Pretzels. Pizza. Buffalo chicken wings. None of these are Code Red Approved.

So just get used to the idea that you're not going to have that gin and tonic for a while. It won't kill you to go without while you're losing weight. If your friends give you a hard time, you can offer to be a designated driver or simply say, "I'm a Rebel."

Drinking Alcohol in Maintenance Mode

Once you move to maintenance mode, it's okay to start drinking alcohol again, if you want to. Of course, you may feel you did just fine without it and decide you don't really need it. Personally, I just don't think it's worth the calories. So I rarely drink. But it's okay if you do. I want to make you aware of some things though, because alcohol is a slippery slope back to being overweight.

Let's talk about wine for a minute, shall we? The medical community recommends that a woman should have one glass of wine per day. Men can have two. (I know, it hardly seems fair, right? We birth the babies, and they get to have more wine!)

Here's the catch, though. Those recommendations are based on a 4- to 5-ounce glass. When someone comes to me for a consultation, I ask them if they drink any alcohol. Most people say yes. Then I ask them how much. They say, "Oh, just one glass."

What they mean by "just one glass" is about 12 ounces. Which is actually 3 glasses according to the recommendations. Go ahead. Pour yourself a "normal" glass of wine, then pour it into a measuring cup and see for yourself! You'll be shocked. It doesn't look like much. Just a typical amount. But it's 3 times more than is recommended. And wine is full of sugar, especially whites and blushes.

Don't get me wrong. I'm not judging how much alcohol you drink. If you choose to drink 3 times the daily limit or a bottle a night, that's your business. You can live your life however you want. Just don't lie to yourself about it. Be honest with yourself, and fully understand what and how much you're putting into your body.

I see so many people beating themselves up because they can't lose weight. They blame themselves. They think there's something wrong with them. They even start to hate their bodies. It breaks my heart because there's nothing wrong with them. Their bodies are working just fine. The problem is the math. They are consuming 3 times more calories than they think they are.

The math is keeping you fat. The math is making you feel crappy. So be honest with yourself. Make sure you truly know how much you are drinking and what that's doing to your weight-loss and maintenance efforts.

Cari Thompson

How Cristy's Sister Faced Her Turning Point, Quit Her Addiction, and Lost 110 Pounds

I'VE NEVER been a thin person. I see people in the Code Red community celebrating "Down to a size 6!" and I just have to laugh and say, "Never was a size 6!" In high school, I hovered around a size 14 or 16 because I loved to eat! And I always blamed my extra weight on being a "bigger girl" or having "big bones." I just figured that's how I was. And it got to the point where 180 turned into 190, which turned into 200. Then a couple of bad relationships, and I was up to 260 pounds in what seemed like a heartbeat.

Weight gain happens insidiously. You don't even realize how big you've gotten until you turn around and you're 100 pounds overweight. Some people have horrible trauma and stress that cause them to gain. For me, though, I was just shoving too much food in my face. I fell for the low-fat, whole-grain lifestyle that society pushes on us.

When my kids were very young, I remember going to Sonic (the best burger place ever!) and getting myself and the kids each a meal—a hamburger, fries, and a giant Coke. I would eat mine, but the kids would only eat a couple of bites. So I would eat theirs too. I would eat like 3,000 calories at a time without even realizing it! That's a great way to get fat. But you don't even notice it happening because you're just busy. I would eat mindlessly and then get on with whatever else I was doing.

MY TURNING POINT

I can remember my turning point like it was yesterday. When my kids were little, we took a family trip to a Six Flags amusement park in California. I love roller coasters, especially the old wooden ones. Now, our society today is pretty accommodating toward heavy people, but that wasn't always the case. Well, I climbed into one of the old-fashioned wooden roller coasters, and I couldn't fasten the seatbelt. I stretched it across my lap and tried to click it in.

No click.

Everyone was watching. I immediately started to sweat, that nervous sweat that trickles down your neck.

My hips were so big, I couldn't wear a roller coaster seatbelt. To make matters worse, the poor kid running the ride came over and tried to assist me. He was lying across me, straining with all his might to click my seatbelt, and he couldn't do it. I felt like this fat girl holding up the ride. I remember that kid trying to push the seatbelt in. He was sweaty and his

dreadlocks were hitting me in the face. My cheeks and my chest got red, and I just flushed with embarrassment. It was utterly humiliating.

Ultimately, he gave up. That seatbelt would not click, so I had to climb back out and exit the ride. Worse, my son had to get out as well because he was too scared to ride by himself. I thought to myself, *I can't even go on rides with my kids anymore.* And I just felt this heavy, sick weight on my heart.

For years, I had done things to deny my weight. I would never look at myself in a full-length mirror. I would check myself from the waist up, just to make sure my hair and makeup were good. I would keep buying bigger sizes, telling myself things like "I'm just a big-boned girl" or "Butts just run bigger in our family." Now that

I've lost 110 pounds, that mirror trick is one way I can tell that I'm starting to creep up again. If I catch myself not looking in full-length mirrors, I know something's off.

I would make excuses for my behavior all the time. I was a nurse working 12-hour shifts, so how would I have time for fitness? I told myself that I could hustle and keep up, it was no big deal. Of course, in your 20s, you can compensate for a while. I could not have managed that work load at that weight if I had been older. I was so heavy that I was running into health issues too. But I denied it and made excuses for it and ignored it. I put it out of my mind—until that day when I couldn't go on a ride with my son. That was my turning point.

Initially, I turned to weight-loss surgery to solve the problem. Unfortunately, I had all sorts of complications, and years later I ended up having more surgeries to reverse the procedure and deal with all the problems it had caused. It did help me lose a little bit of weight in the beginning. But **IT DID NOT ADDRESS THE REAL PROBLEM**—that I was addicted to diet soda and sugar. This surgery cost a lot of money and pain that I could have avoided if I had just paid attention to my sister.

I remember talking to a woman at church who had recently lost a lot of weight. I asked her for her secret. She looked at me and said, "Cari, it was just my time. Maybe now isn't your time, but it will be." She was very sweet about it. At the time I thought she was just patronizing me. But afterward, it really hit me.

It was my time.

I took that, dialed my life in, and lost the weight.

EVERYBODY HAS A DIFFERENT TURNING POINT

What I want you to take away from this is that everybody has a turning point, and it doesn't have to be 110 pounds. Your turning point could be not fitting into your favorite jeans. Your turning point could be 20 pounds. Or a photo where you don't even recognize yourself anymore. Don't think for a minute that you have to be obese before you have a turning point. It could be that you had a baby and are struggling with losing the pregnancy weight. That is a turning point too.

If you've tried countless shakes, diets, and pills, it is definitely your time. I used to spend money on thermogenics, and take a pill 3 times a day, I was so desperate. That was not the right plan, and it was not the right time. My right time was when I couldn't ride a roller coaster with my son.

FACING MY SWEETNESS ADDICTION

The biggest truth I had to face was that I was completely and helplessly addicted to sugar and diet soda. The biggest lie our society tells us is that "diet" drinks won't affect you the same way sugar does. Baloney! When I was drinking that stuff,

I was hungry and thirsty *all the time.* And I tried everything to lose weight. I drank the shakes. I took the fen-phen. I went to all the weight-loss meetings. Nothing worked until I listened to Cristy.

When I finally quit drinking diet soda, I felt like a junkie coming off narcotics. I work as a nurse in the intensive care unit, and I see what it's like when people come off meth and heroin with the tremors and nausea and the headaches. It was that bad.

It's amazing the number of chemicals that are leaving your body. You really have to be prepared for that and decide that taking your life back is more important than ever drinking another diet soda or eating real food. And now I weigh less than I did in high school.

It's amazing to be able to buy the clothes that I want to wear, and look at myself in

If you're sick of how you feel, how you look, or you're facing weight-related health issues, this might very well be your time.

another bland piece of bread. It doesn't matter if you weigh 120 pounds and only want to lose 5, or you're 260 like I was and need to lose a heck of a lot more—the addiction is the same! I didn't start to heal until I faced that fact the the diet soda and the sugar were killing me.

Now, I was lucky because Cristy is my sister and when I finally decided it was my time, she was right there to help me. But that doesn't mean I got off easy. I had to follow the rules the same way everyone else does. She got on my case every time I started to stray, even when I was in the hospital having surgery! Thank goodness the rules are simple. I stopped drinking diet sodas. I started drinking water. I ate

a full-length mirror. Sometimes I'll catch a glimpse of my reflection in a glass window and think, "Who's that pretty girl?" Then I realize it's me! No matter how much or how little you need to lose—you can absolutely do it with Code Red.

It's so exciting when it's your time, and the best part is **YOU GET TO DECIDE** when that is. It can be right now!

Are We There Yet? Travel Tips

WOO HOO! ROAD TRIP!

Who doesn't love to spend hours in a cramped metal box with a lot of other cranky people just counting the minutes until they get to their destination? No matter how much you're looking forward to traveling to visit friends or family, or just to get out of town for a while, there's no denying that the actual trip can be a challenge. Especially if you're trying to eat clean.

Here's the good news—there's nothing to be afraid of, as long as you plan ahead. Whether you're taking a car trip or traveling by plane, train, or pack mule, there are lots of healthy options for you. The key is to pre-pack your food.

If you're traveling by car, you can pack your food in a cooler. If you're going by plane, you can still pack it in a cooler bag; you just have to limit your liquids before you go through security. Let me share a few options.

You can slice up veggies ahead of time—carrots, celery, cucumbers, bell peppers, tomatoes, mushrooms—whatever you like. If they tend to get slimy, like cucumbers, don't slice them up until the last minute. You can add some

THE CODE RED REVOLUTION

fats like natural almond butter or cream cheese to put on top of the veggies. If you're in maintenance mode, bring small cups of hummus to dip them into.

For protein, you can cook up steak or chicken breasts and slice them into bite-sized pieces. Sometimes I roll the slices into lettuce wraps and bag them. They're easy to hold onto, and they're not messy. So they make great snacks or full meals. I also sometimes pack salami slices or pre-packaged tuna. You can dump a couple scoops of protein powder into a blender bottle and add water when you're on the road.

I also put raw nuts like pecans, almonds, walnuts, and sunflower seeds into little 1-ounce bags. I might also include small portions of dark chocolate. It's easy to go overboard on these, so pre-measuring is important.

Now you might say, "Cristy, that's not very much." You don't need very much. The biggest reason people eat in the car or on a plane is because they're bored, not because they're hungry. Don't eat more than you need.

A huge part of a healthy travel plan is making sure you have something to do. How will you keep your mind occupied in the car and the hotel room? Bring a book, watch a movie on your iPad, play with a coloring book, knit a sweater— whatever! Just keep your mind off food. And that goes for the kids too. If they're happily listening to an audiobook, they're not going to bug you for a milkshake. You won't be stopping at every other exit. You'll save money. You'll save time. And you'll stay on plan.

You'll still need to weigh yourself every morning. So you'll need a scale to do it. The ones my clients use are compact travel scales, which are about $25 on Amazon. They're about the size of a flat notebook, fit in a backpack easily, and work great. Sometimes when the surface beneath the scale changes, your weight will get wonky. You might be up 7 pounds or down 4 with no reason

260

other than the fact that you're weighing in a different environment. Don't worry about it. Just keep up the habit.

Definitely also bring a food scale and measuring spoons with you. Even if you don't use them when you eat out, you'll want to measure the cream in your coffee in the morning. Speaking of eating out while you travel, can you arrange to do at least some of your own cooking? If not, can you catch a taxi to the local grocery store and pick up a few things like guacamole cups, tuna packets, precooked bacon, and almonds? If you plan ahead, you can make at least 1 or 2 meals in your hotel room. Not only will you stay on plan, but you'll also save some serious money.

Don't be afraid of traveling. It just takes a little bit of preparation on your part, and you won't miss those stale airplane pretzels one little bit.

NO TEST, NO TESTIMONY

I have a new private program client named Sarah. She started off on Day One by going on spring vacation with her family. She watched my instructional video, and she had her program book in hand. Armed with only those and no experience, she packed off with her family to California.

And you know what? She nailed it! She lost 2 pounds a day. You know how hard it is to stay on track on the road, and believe me, she was tested. She watched her family eat pizza, brownies, and all kinds of stuff she knew she couldn't have. Did she cheat? No. She left the room if she had to, but she stayed on track the entire time.

What happened when she got home? She was back on her home turf. She was back to *her* pantry, *her* grocery store, *her* schedule, *her* kitchen. She jumped in with both feet and came back victorious. That vacation was her test, and her new body is her testimony.

Every time you go through a tough situation, it gives you strength. If there's birthday cake in your office, that's a test. Don't eat it, and you get to drive home knowing you were tested and are stronger for it. And the more tests you pass, the easier the next one becomes.

Another client of mine, Heather, went on a vacation to Maui. Another perfect opportunity to get off track and eat foods that set her back. Heather didn't cave though. She stayed on track the whole time, and came home with minimal recovery needed. She didn't let being out of her normal environment derail her goals. Any time you travel out of town or go on vacation, you are tested. Every time you stick to the plan, it strengthens your testimony.

Ever heard of Cesar Milan, the Dog Whisperer? If you've ever seen his show, you can tell he loved it when he got a difficult dog. When those dogs start acting up and making a big fuss, he enjoyed it because it was a challenge. He loved to figure out that dog's angle and help its owner learn how to handle it.

I love being tested. When your kid has a birthday party, or you have a conference out of state—those are the times when you can test your mettle. And I *love* watching you come out on top. That's one big difference between you and the folks on the *Biggest Loser*. Those people have a team of trainers and chefs, and they're all isolated on a ranch where they don't have to face any temptations. They're not in the real world.

You are.

The real world is full of parties, conferences, and food-centered holidays. Your successes mean more because *you* succeeded despite what real life threw at you. I had a guy steal $36,000 from me. I lived with another guy who beat me up. But I survived, and I am better than ever. Those were tests I passed, and my success means more because of them. The real world throws you curveballs. It gives you challenges you didn't expect and maybe didn't deserve.

But you are up to the challenge. And you will be stronger for facing it head on. Every one you survive is a notch in your belt. So don't dread your tests.

Don't ask, "Why me?"

Say, "Try me!"

You and I, we've got this. We can handle anything. I am with you the whole way.

Whatever life throws your way, you can overcome it. You can be stronger. Face your tests, and your testimony will be all the stronger for it.

22 Holiday and Birthday Baking Tips

LOVE TO BAKE? Love to snack while you bake? If so, you're not alone.

Be honest, do half the chocolate chips wind up in your mouth? Do you sneak the candied pecans or peanut butter cups while you're waiting for the next batch of cookies to come out of the oven? Do you lick the beaters?

If you are worried about eating while you are baking, I've got a great tip for you. Bleach your teeth. Put the bleach trays or strips in your mouth, and bleach your teeth while you're baking. You cannot eat or drink anything while the bleaching trays are in your mouth. It takes about an hour to do it. That's about as long as it will take you to bake something from start to finish. If you are worried about nibbling, this is a really good deterrent.

You can also keep your mouth occupied with a stick of gum. Or maybe even a toothpick. Just put something else in there that will keep you from nibbling while you bake. (I know, you're just "testing" it, right?)

THE CODE RED REVOLUTION

How Do You Measure Up?

Another problem with baking, and cooking in general, is measuring. Don't get complacent with your measuring. For butter, oil, or anything else. Use a measuring device and level it off. One level tablespoon of butter is not the same as a heaping tablespoon that you just cut right off the stick.

There may not be a big difference in how your recipes turn out, but there's a HUGE difference in calorie counts. I've seen it over and over with my clients. They completely sabotage their efforts because they're doubling or tripling their calories with bad measuring. (Once again—the math is working against you.)

The same goes for chocolate chips, sprinkles, and any other sugar-laden dessert decorations. I'm not suggesting that you count the number of chips you use, or that you deprive your cupcakes of that perfect frosting. But be aware that those things have calories. Be honest with yourself. And maybe consider cutting down the amount of decorating you do—or skipping it altogether. Would you enjoy those cookies just as much if they didn't have a sugar glaze? It's entirely possible.

Great Grandma Would Be Proud

Another strategy is to change your recipe. I know, that's sacrilege for some people. That rum cake recipe has been in the family for generations. Well, what about this generation? And the generations to come? How cool would it be if they used *your* recipe—one that didn't pack on the pounds every year?

There are some really smart people who have already figured out how to lower the sugar and carbs in your favorite recipes. Just google them: "low-carb brownies" or "healthy birthday cake." It might be as simple as learning how to bake with almond flour instead of the regular all-purpose variety. And who knows, you might like these healthier versions even better than Great-Great-Grandma Edith's recipe. Besides, she would be happy that you're taking care of yourself.

Free Up Some Time (and Get a Massage)

Some people love to have a few special treats around, but actually hate baking. Is that you? Then don't bake! Save yourself the time and the dirty dishes. Let yourself off the hook. You could put that time to much better use—like a spa day! Just don't rely on your grocery store bakery for those treats, because who knows what they've put in those pasty-white concoctions?! Find a bakery that specializes in using natural ingredients and just order the Christmas cookies this year.

Here's an idea—find a friend (or a child) who does love to bake and ask them to make you a healthier version of your favorites. There are plenty of low-sugar, low-carb versions of everything from pie to brownies to sugar cookies. Offer to buy the ingredients and maybe even pay them for their time. You get exactly what you want without all the hassle of baking.

Timing is Everything

Look, I'm all for doing the work ahead of time to save on stress later. But baking cookies days ahead of a special occasion is just asking for trouble. If you know those suckers are sitting in the cupboard, how long do you think you can realistically hold out before you have "just one"? (Or more like the whole damn batch!)

Even if you're some sort of superhero and manage to avoid the temptation, chances are pretty good your family won't. Then all the cookies will be gone, and you'll have to make a whole bunch more for whatever special occasion you were saving them for.

Save yourself the trouble and the temptation—save the baking until the last minute. Don't even shop for the ingredients until it's time to bake (because damn, those chocolate chips taste good right out of the bag!)

23 A Parent's Job is Never Done

THE FOOTBALL GAME WENT LATE. Band practice starts at 6 a.m. Your daughter's dance team made All-State and you're the chaperone. Parents... you are amazing creatures! Really. I am always *so* impressed with how you juggle everything you have to do in a day. And that doesn't even include your regular work schedules. It's no wonder so many moms and dads are overweight and stressed out. There's just no time!

The good news is you already know you can handle whatever life throws at you. You are a master at juggling schedules and making sure everything is handled. So now you just have to shift focus a little bit and give *yourself* the same love and care you give your kids. I have a lot of clients who are parents, some of them with 3 or more little ones at home. And we've gotten really good at figuring out how to make the Code Red Lifestyle work, even when you're running around 24/7.

We've already talked about a ton of strategies for sticking to the rules. The biggest thing I want to say here is that you deserve to be healthy. You deserve to feel amazing and have more energy. You deserve to feel sexy and desirable!

Once you make the decision that you are a Rebel, that you're going to do this no matter what, I know you'll make it happen. Preparation is key. Sure, the unexpected is commonplace for you. But you can always be prepared with almonds and water bottles in the car, or pre-made meals in the fridge. You've got enough stress in your day. Let your meals be simple and easy.

Sleep is one of the biggest hurdles for my clients with children. It has to be a priority. And maybe you've gotten used to functioning on very little sleep. You may not even realize how little sleep you're getting. Start paying attention. Keep a sleep log and notice your patterns. How can you get creative and make sure you're getting those 7–8 hours a night? I know, you're laughing at me right now. But try, okay? There's not much that's more beneficial to your good health than sleep.

Julie Anne Eason

Put Herself First and Lost 67 Pounds in 6 Months

AS A MOTHER, I have always put my family first, no matter what. My time was theirs, and I focused all my energy on their care. I was never focused on myself because there was always someone else to take care of. Even though I've been heavy since college, I was always told that I carried it well. People would tell me that I didn't look like I was as heavy as I was, but I can tell you, my weight *hurt*.

As I got older and my weight crept higher and higher, I found I was in more and more pain. My knees hurt, my ankles hurt, and it kept me from doing things I wanted to do. I loved skiing, ice-skating, and dancing, but it hurt to do them. I pushed

through the pain because I'm stubborn that way, but it wasn't fun. I knew I could do everything better, if I could just get rid of the weight.

But I was a working mom, so I pushed those feelings down and just didn't think about them because I had other people to take care of. I am good at focusing on other things and distracting myself from what I don't want to feel. So I focused on my family and I threw myself into my work. I am a writer and publisher, so I would literally sit in front of my computer and not move except to go to the refrigerator. I told myself that I wanted to be successful in my work, and that success came at the expense of my body.

My turning point was not a big, dramatic thing. There was no real defining moment. I didn't have that big epiphany standing in front of the mirror or something like that. The year my youngest graduated from high school, I just realized it was time. It was finally time for me to take care of myself.

That's it.

FINDING THE RIGHT TOOLS

I first discovered Code Red when I saw a friend of mine who had lost 60 pounds after working with Cristy one-on-one. I took one look at her and said, "I want that!" I just couldn't believe how fast she lost all that weight. That was when I knew I had to do it for myself. It was like, "If she can do it, I can do it. I don't know who this Cristy chick is, but I'm gonna find out."

When I met Cristy, I immediately connected with her because she's a fighter. I practice a particularly violent martial art myself, and the fact that Cristy was a boxer really helped me to connect with her on a personal level. It's like we have a similar background.

Now, having been overweight for almost 30 years, I have tried every diet, plan, and product out there. I never made a lot of

was that those were not the first things Cristy emphasized.

She emphasized sleep. She emphasized water. She emphasized not exercising. That was amazing, I was like, "Wait, I don't have to exercise, and I'm still going to lose weight?" It was a little bit unbelievable, but I had seen the proof.

THE MAGIC SWITCH

When I decided to try it, I was still really skeptical that I could go the distance because I had done so many other things before and had not been able to stick with them. I'd been overweight for more than 25 years. All that time, I thought there was some magic thing that would work and change my life.

It turned out there was no magic thing. The magic thing was my brain deciding that it was my turn and that this was going to happen!

That is the beauty of this program, that you flip a switch and you become a new person. All the strategies work together, but in the end, it's your mind that makes the decision.

I used to think *Oh, I'm losing weight this week, but it's not going to last.* Or *I lost ten pounds, but it'll come back, I won't keep*

progress though. I think that was because I couldn't stick with whatever I was doing. I wasn't able to sustain any of those programs for more than a few weeks.

The Code Red Lifestyle had elements to it that I knew to be true, like cutting out sugar, eating a high-fat and low-carb diet. I knew those things were true, and I had seen other people lose weight that way. But what really surprised me *this up.* But I worked through that, and I stopped listening to those voices in my head. When you work through those negative thoughts and you have hundreds of others cheering you on—you flip a switch and suddenly, you can do it!

At this point, I am about halfway through my program. I have lost 67 pounds and I have another 35 to lose. The beautiful thing about this is, I know I can make it. This is for real.

My big test came right at the beginning. I had just started with Cristy, and I went on vacation to England. Fortunately, I had the most amazing support from my husband. He would say things like, "I know you can have this, but do you really want it?" Every day he would tell me I was doing great, and that he was so proud of me. I was on vacation in a foreign country, and I wanted to eat all the things! I wanted the pastries and the steak pie, you know? But I didn't. I didn't cheat once that whole week. I was tempted, but I knew what I could eat and I knew what I couldn't. And I lost weight every day while I was over there.

I travel a lot for work too, but that is no longer an issue. I know that I can be successful and stay on track even when I'm traveling. I bring my own food to the airports, and I know how to eat right when I am away from home. It's just become a normal thing. I haven't cheated once in 6 months, as far as food goes. Sometimes I get behind on my water, and that is frustrating to me because it's an easy thing.

THE PAIN JUST DISAPPEARED

Besides losing weight, there are other victories to celebrate. The first thing I noticed was my joints stopped hurting. That was huge. Before I started working with Cristy, I was to the point that it even hurt to walk some days. I figured I was just getting older, or maybe I was getting arthritis or whatever. But now I know my joints were inflamed because I was eating sugar. When I stopped, it only took a few days for the pain to disappear. Just a few days without sugar, and I was walking down the stairs and I was like, "Holy crap, my knees don't hurt!"

Not too long ago, I went shopping in a store that I used to take my teenage girls to. I had always hated going there because I could never fit into anything, so I had to just sit there while my daughters tried on all these really cute clothes. But recently, I went in there on a whim, found a cute pair of jeans, and they fit me! It felt so cool to fit into clothing that wasn't from a plus-size store. For me, that was a huge victory, to see something that looked cute on a hanger and also looked cute on me.

nothing hurts. My energy level is higher than it has been in years.

So if you're reading this story, and the other stories, just know that they're real.

That is the switch you can make when you are around people who are so strong and so convinced you can do it. When you are around people like the Code Red community who believe in you so much, something happens in your brain that allows you to believe in yourself.

I have improved in my martial art as well. I've been able to enter tournaments again and do really well. I was really competitive when I was younger, but then I stopped going to practice, and didn't participate at the level that I used to. I could still play, but it wasn't as much fun. Now that I'm thinner and able to be more athletic, I am having more fun with it. I go to the gym not to lose weight but because I feel like it. I can run on the treadmill and

We're all real people, and we were all skeptical at the beginning. I remember at first I thought this couldn't possibly be true. I'll never see results like these other people. But we all did it. It is true, and we're never going back.

You may have tried everything out there or exercised until you wanted to puke, and you may have given up.

But try this. Give it a try, and you will be astounded at how strong you can be. If you do, make sure you join the community because that's where you'll find that magic brain switch. Once that happens, you'll find strength and courage you never knew you had.

You can do this. I believe in you!

24 Tough Love Time

LIFE CAN BE MESSY.

Everyone has problems they don't deserve, circumstances that nobody should have to deal with. Every day, people lose loved ones, or face trouble at work. People lose houses, lose their jobs, get divorced.

You have read my own life story, so you know that I know how unfair life can be. With that in mind, believe me when I say you cannot ever go back to eating the way you did before. It sounds harsh, but believe me, your old habits failed you. If you are facing pre-diabetes or type II, if your knees ache from your excess weight, or you can't run around with your children or grandchildren, your old habits failed you miserably.

No matter how difficult your life is right now, trying to soothe yourself with junk food will only make your life worse. When times are hard, your body needs wholesome and nutritious food more than ever.

When you begin to follow the Code Red Lifestyle, you learn how to eat and how to heal your body. You can't go back from there, no matter what happens. It could be that you used to handle stress with food. Or perhaps it was

THE CODE RED REVOLUTION

THE POWER OF HABITS

I highly recommend reading *The Power of Habit*, by Charles Duhigg. It will change your whole understanding of why we do what we do out of habit, and why they are so difficult to change. Smoking, drinking too much, or stopping by Dairy Queen twice a week—they're all habits. And by definition, that means they are unconscious actions. Like, your brain actually stops thinking (to some extent) when you repeat a habitual action. It takes far less energy to simply run a routine over and over again than to make the individual decisions each time. Have you ever found yourself halfway through a bag of chips and then thought to yourself *What am I doing?*

We are habitual beings, to the point where we're not even aware of them. When people realize they have an unhealthy habit, they think they can just stop it. But that usually doesn't work because you're already finished by the time you realize you're into another habitual action.

One of my habits is having afternoon coffee. For years, around 3 p.m. I would take out the French press and make myself an afternoon coffee. There is nothing especially bad about coffee. In moderation, coffee is a healthy level of caffeine. The problem with my habit wasn't the coffee. It was the whipping cream I put in it. For my body, having cream in my coffee twice a day was too much dairy. I wanted to be leaner, and

sadness, some void you felt in yourself that you had to fill. I can't stress this fact enough: Managing your emotions with food is not the answer, and never will be.

You and I, we are Rebels! We don't need that garbage to deal with what life throws at us. We care about ourselves too much to poison our bodies with carbs and sugar. The negative results from binging on junk will long outlast what is a brief and empty high.

the calories in that whipping cream were taking up too much of my daily allowance. So I took a look at the *real* reason I drank coffee in the afternoon, and discovered I just really liked that hot, comforting drink. It wasn't the coffee, it was the relaxing break in the middle of my day. Then I realized I didn't need to drink coffee. I could replace that habit with a different one.

So I switched to tea. I bought myself a cute little teacup and saucer, and a pretty teapot to match. Both made me feel good. I don't put cream in my tea, but the preparation is similar to the French-pressed coffee. To my brain, it feels the same. At the same time every afternoon, I set a pot of water to boil and I have my hot drink. All I did was replace the coffee and cream with tea and a pinch of stevia. My habit is still to have a hot drink every afternoon, I just switched what that drink was.

If you have a habit that you want to change, try replacing it with a different habit. Maybe your family has ice cream every Sunday, and your weight is creeping up. Consider switching to a lower calorie alternative, or taking a family trip to the movies instead. Whatever you do, it will be easier to replace the habit with a different one rather than to try and cancel it altogether.

If life has you stressed out, do something good for yourself. Walk your dog, meet a friend for a movie, meditate, paint, go to the driving range—anything to help you to your happy place. Anything but empty calories. You are too strong for that now.

Love yourself, and be tough.

You Got This!

THANKS FOR STICKING WITH ME THROUGH THIS BOOK. I hope I've encouraged you and shown you that this year does not have to be like every other one. It doesn't have to end in a 10-pound weight gain. It doesn't have to be a giant sleep-deprived stressfest.

You now have the tools you need to lose as much weight as you want and to keep it off for good. Not just for a few weeks in January when you're "motivated," but for birthdays, soccer season, vacations, business travel, and weddings—any special occasions, or no special occasion at all. These tools work for your life!

The rules are simple:

1. Sleep at least 7–8 hours every night.

2. Drink at least one gallon of water per day.

3. Weigh yourself every morning.

4. Don't eat past 6:30 p.m.

5. Weigh, measure, and log everything that goes into your mouth.

6. Keep the junk out of your house.

7. Follow the Foods to Eat/Foods to Avoid list.

You know what? It doesn't matter who you are. It doesn't matter whether you're rich or poor, old or young. It doesn't matter if you work behind a desk or on the docks. Every single person can do this. This is not just for athletes, this is not just for celebrities. It's for all of us. And we are all in this together.

I use these strategies myself. My clients use them, as well as my friends and family. This book is the result of hundreds of nutrition plans and participants who have all had to get through the same daily challenges that you do. I have walked down this path myself, and I've helped others walk it too. Real people from every walk of life are losing weight while enjoying fun-filled (and dealing with stress-filled) daily lives. And I'm telling you it's gonna work for you, too.

You got this. I just know it!

Take care of yourself. Because you deserve it.

Cristy "Code Red"

P.S. Remember our deal?

Back in the introduction, I asked you to give me a chance to prove to you how well this revolutionary way of eating works. Now it's time for you to go out and try it for yourself. Then, please share this book! Review it. Talk about it.

I can't make a revolution happen by myself. It takes people. Lots of people. Together, we can change the world.

Appendix

This book is an easy way to dive into the Code Red Lifestyle. If you'd like to learn even more about the science behind high-fat, low-carb eating or sugar addiction, I recommend the following:

Documentaries

Food, Inc.

Fed Up

Hungry For Change

Food Matters

That Sugar Film

Books

Wheat Belly: Lose the Wheat, Lose the Weight, and Find Your Path Back to Health. By William Davis, M.D.

Grain Brain: The Surprising Truth About Wheat, Carbs, and Sugar— Your Brain's Silent Killers. By David Perlmutter, M.D. with Kristin Loberg

Acknowledgments

MOM & DAD: Thank you for covering me with prayer. Your prayers have kept me safe, alive, and blessed over the past 41 years. I've inherited spiritual gifts and generational blessings from you, and no one will ever know the countless hours you've spent on your knees interceding for me.

ABE JACKSON: Years ago when I sat in your bank office, I was broke, broken, damaged, and sad. You didn't look down on me. You didn't laugh at me. You didn't treat me as less of a person. You helped me repair my credit and build up wealth, and cheered me on each year as my business grew. You believed in me even when I didn't believe it was possible.

NANCY: The administrator at the Orofino Care Center in Orofino, ID, when I worked there in 1991 and 1992. You'll never know how much it meant to me when you sat in the break room that one day and spoke to me with such kindness. I was 15 years old. You smiled warmly and told me I would make a great nurse someday. I was on top of the world and I've never forgotten that day.

JULIE EASON: Thank you for making this whole journey painless and easy.

NIC GERMANO/JIMMY BLANN: Thank you for training me for free when I was first learning to box. I was broke, but you took your time and effort each evening to train me. You saw the potential of a future world-class pro athlete.

About the Author

Cristy "Code Red" Nickel is an author, speaker, and celebrity nutritionist. She has been in the health and fitness industry since 1994, helping people lose weight by eating real food. Her weight-loss program has helped thousands of people lose weight without hunger, exercise, shakes, pills, or diet food.

In 2003, Cristy became a federally licensed professional boxer and fought in 15 professional fights all over the world. She was named one of the "Top 3 Most Dangerous Females on the Planet" by *Ring Magazine*, which landed her a coaching role on MTV's hit series *MADE*. The success of that show propelled her to New York City to train top celebrities, business tycoons, models, and professional athletes. In 2008, Cristy was awarded "New York's Best Trainer" by *Allure* magazine.

For more information about Cristy "Code Red" Nickel or her weight-loss programs, please visit **CODEREDLIFESTYLE.COM**

Code Red Corporate Wellness Programs

Bring the Code Red Lifestyle to your office with a specialized program. Improving employee health can contribute to fewer sick days, better productivity, and higher company morale. For more information on setting up a program for your office contact:

Corporate@CodeRedLifestyle.com

Law Office Loses 114.8 Pounds in 6 Weeks: Better Health and Higher Morale

The challenge has brought so much energy and excitement to our firm. It's really brought the employees together with a newfound camaraderie. We talk to each other about the Code Red Lifestyle every morning, supporting and congratulating each other. Even though it's a competition, we're all excited for each other's wins. —**MARCIA, DIRECTOR OF ADMINISTRATION**

I would recommend a Code Red Corporate program to any company that wants to help its employees improve their health, reduce absenteeism, and just build a happier, more productive workplace. —**NATASHA HAZLETT, ATTORNEY**

I so appreciated the support from Cristy and the company as a whole. One of the biggest benefits for me was that I no longer dread company meetings. Our office manager made sure we had Code Red Approved snacks. Not only that, but our office kitchen got cleaned up and all the junk is out of there! —**MACHELLE, PARALEGAL**

My experience was fantastic. I really liked the team effort. The first 2 weeks with no sugar or carbs was pretty rough. But knowing that others in the office were going through it with me made it so much better. When I faced difficult days, I had the support and understanding of my co-workers. It's funny, I've had to double our water order for the office! —**AMANDA, ADMINISTRATIVE ASSISTANT**

I recommend the corporate program to any business that wants to inspire its employees lose weight and live healthier lives. —**GRANT, COMPTROLLER**

Index

Numbers

A

B

as energy, 118

filling up on, 168

food recommendations, 82

healthy types, 26–27

and protein, 108

reducing intake, 81–82

storing, 24

types, 81

fat-free craze, 82

"fat-free" foods, 84

Fed Up, 70

fen-phen, 107

fiber, 118–119

fish, 168, 220

flaxseed oil, 83

folate, 119

food. *See also* comfort food; eating

adding back in, 202–204

changing relationship with, 211

as fuel, 210–211

measuring, 266

Party Survival Guide, 74

presentation, 240

as reward, 210

weighing, measuring, and logging, 143, 154–158, 187–190, 197, 281

food diary, keeping, 73. *See also* video diary

food intake, limiting, 108

food labels, 82, 132, 134

"food products," 133

food scale, 73, 154, 157, 188, 198, 244, 260

Foods to Eat/Foods to Avoid, 143, 160–162, 281

frozen vegetables, 134. *See also* vegetables

fructose, 203

fructose sweetener, 72

fruit juice, 72

fruits, 74, 132, 162, 166, 168, 202–203

fuel, food as, 210–211

Fulcher Koontz, Sheli, 38

fullness, feeling, 148

Future You, 44, 46

G

ghee, 83

Gilligan Scenario, 26–28. *See also* desert islands

gimmicks, 105–106, 109

glucose, 24–26, 70. *See also* A1C; blood sugar level; sugars

gluten. *See also* protein

cutting out, 91

explained, 89

problems, 90

"gluten-free" label, 82

goal weight. *See also* line in the sand

achieving, 63, 188–189

determining, 129–132

goals of weight-loss programs, 110

grains, cutting out, 91, 162, 166

Greek traditional yogurt, 162, 219–220, 239

guarana, 107

H

habits, power of, 278

Hafliger, Sara, 224

hair health, improving, 149